*Sunday Savers:*
*Sharing Fun!* – 2018 Sharing Time Activities

# *Theme: I Am a Child of God*

• 18 Learning Activities to Match Monthly Themes—Plus Bookmark

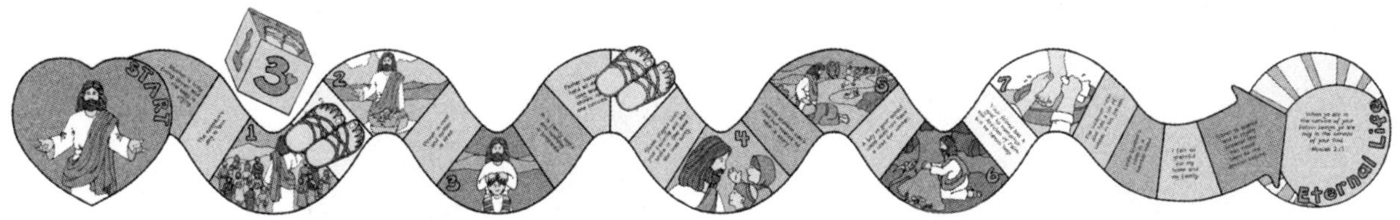


Sample ACTIVITY: *I Will Follow Jesus—Service Road Game* (shown above)—Use For: September week 1 Lesson "Jesus taught us how to serve others."

"I Am a Child of God" bookmarks (shown right p. 138)

***No CD-ROM is available for these images. You can purchase colored DOWNLOADS from GospelGrabBag.com.***

***MORE FROM Mary H. Ross, Author, and Jennette Guymon-King, Illustrator:***

. ***Primary Teachers:*** Don't miss the ***Sunday Savers*** books and CD-ROMs with an activity for every lesson in the 2018

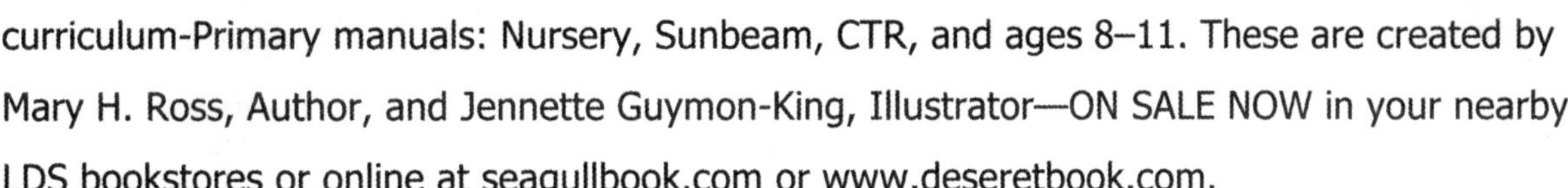

curriculum-Primary manuals: Nursery, Sunbeam, CTR, and ages 8–11. These are created by Mary H. Ross, Author, and Jennette Guymon-King, Illustrator—ON SALE NOW in your nearby LDS bookstores or online at seagullbook.com or www.deseretbook.com.

. ***Primary Leaders:***

DOWNLOAD from gospelgrabbag.com:

(1) "I Am a Child of God" monthly theme scripture posters and cards,

(2) Activity Days activities for every goal, (3) Articles of Faith 1–13 scripture posters and more

. ***Primary Music Leaders:***

DOWNLOAD from gospelgrabbag.com: (1) Song Visuals to teach practice songs,

(2) Singing Activities to motivate children to sing

## About the AUTHOR, ILLUSTRATOR:

Mary H. Ross, author, and Jennette Guymon-King, illustrator, have sold over one million LDS products published by Covenant Communications. This is the 19th year for this Sharing Time book.

Mary H. Ross, Author

Jennette Guymon-King, Illustrator

***No CD-ROM is available to print the images in this book in color. You can purchase DOWNLOADS from GospelGrabBag.com.***

---

*At **GospelGrabBag.com** you can:*

1. DOWNLOAD "I Am a Child of God" monthly theme posters and song visuals.
2. DOWNLOAD Activity Days activities for every goal with a matching invitation.
3. PREVIEW the Sunday Savers series of books and CD-ROMs for Nursery, Sunbeam, CTR, and ages 8-11. You will find an activity for every lesson in the 2018 manuals. Purchase at LDS bookstores or DeseretBook.com or SeagullBook.com.

---

**QUIZ-BEE FAN DECKS** are found at LDS bookstores or online: Book of Mormon Quiz-Bee. Articles of Faith Quiz-Bee. These are ideal gifts for children, missionaries, and adults.

---



PUBLISHER: Covenant Communications, Inc., American Fork, Utah—First printing: November 2017

***Sunday Savers™ Sharing Fun: I Am a Child of God***

978-1-52440-514-4

---



*Acknowledgment:* Lettering Delights, www.letteringdelights.com for fonts.

# INTRODUCTION

## SHARING FUN—Sharing Time Activities
## 2018 Theme: I Am a Child of God

This volume of teaching ideas is designed for the 2018 Primary Sharing Time theme. Plus, it can be used year after year for family home evening lessons and Sharing Time themes that help children come to learn and say, **"I am a child of God."**

You will find 20 learning activities (one or two for every month of the year). Each is designed to present on a poster or board with visuals large enough for children to see and visualize the lessons taught.

Each coordinates with the **"I Am a Child of God"** theme for that week/month. Example shown is the Keeping Inside the Fence (Commandments Keep Us Safe QUIZ) activity for February Sharing Time.

***TO USE THE Sharing Fun! BOOK:*** Copy the visuals, color, cut out, and follow instructions.

***No CD-ROM is available for these images. You can purchase colored DOWNLOADS from GospelGrabBag.com.***

***THEME BOOKMARK:*** Don't miss the "I AM A CHILD OF GOD" girl and boy bookmark p. 138-9 that can be given to children this year.

**FOR SINGING LEADERS:** Song visuals to help teach the 2018 practice songs are available to download/print from gospelgrabbag.com (sample shown right for the February theme: When We Choose the Right, We Are Blessed).

**SCRIPTURE MEMORIZATION:** Monthly theme scriptures for the 2018 year are available to download/print from gospelgrabbag.com. They are in large posters or small cards to give children (sample shown left to match with February's Sharing Time theme).

**LET CHILDREN TEACH:** Older children can present the ideas for Sharing Time. **BEST OF ALL:** You can enjoy these activities for monthly family home evenings.

Don't miss the **Articles of Faith 1-13** scripture posters and cards to print from GospelGrabBag.com.

# 2018 Sharing Time Activities:
## *Theme: I Am a Child of God*
## *TABLE OF CONTENTS*

## JANUARY Theme: I Am a Child of God, and He Has a Plan for Me

### *PRACTICE TIME:*

. **SCRIPTURE MEMORIZATION—Romans 8:16** (shown left). Posters and cards are available to download from GospelGrabBag.com.
. **PRACTICE SONG—Sing "I Am a Child of God"** (*Children's Songbook*, 2–3) using the song visuals (shown right). These are available to download from GospelGrabBag.com.

### *SHARING TIME, Week 1: Heavenly Father's plan is a plan of happiness.*

### *ACTIVITY: Plan of Happiness: Premortal, Mortal, and Postmortal Life MATCH GAME*

**OBJECTIVE:** Teach children or have youth teach children about preearth life, earth life, and postmortal life as they follow Heavenly Father's plan of happiness. With each, they will learn that God knows and loves them.
**TO MAKE:** Copy, color, and cut out the images that follow. Make three copies of the smiley faces. Mount the word strips on the backs of the faces. Laminate. Use tape or magnets to mount visuals.
**ACTIVITY:**
1. Place the images on the board and the faces around the room. Tell children/youth you are thinking of someone who loves us, who knows each one of us by name. He knows what we are thinking, and He wants us to be happy. He has a plan for us. Who is this? Our Heavenly Father. Have children repeat, "God is my Heavenly Father. He knows and loves me."
2. Sing, "I Will Follow God's Plan," in the *Children's Songbook*, 164.
3. Divide children into teams to play the match game. Point to the premortal world and say, "We lived in heaven before we came to earth. Many things happened there. We made many choices. Now we live in mortal life. The choices we make here will determine the life we will have in the postmortal world. Let's ponder the three stages of life and see if we know what happened and what will happen in each to live Heavenly Father's plan of happiness."
4. Have children take turns choosing a smiley face; the leader reads the question. The child then makes a match by placing the smiley face under the stage of life where it belongs. If playing in teams to compete, give points for each area in which they post, taking turns: premortal (1 point), mortal (2 points) and postmortal (3 points).

Premortal Life

Mortal Life

Postmortal Life

Make 3 copies.

My life began here in this spirit world, where Heavenly Father created my spirit.

This is where I first heard about Heavenly Father's plan of happiness.

Here I chose to follow Jesus and make righteous choices.

Here Jesus Christ volunteered to be our Savior.

My life here has a purpose: to learn to choose the right.

Here I will work and pray and learn to be like Jesus. I will follow God's plan for me.

While living here, I will pray to seek God's light to direct my choices.

Here our spirit was united with a physical body so we can become like Heavenly Father and Jesus Christ.

We are told that while living here, we must live by faith, not seeing God. But we can talk to Him in prayer.

This life is a test to see if we can learn to live God's commandments.

While living here, we can receive God's sacred ordinances, like baptism and marrying in the temple.

In this place, we can experience joy, sorrow, pain, and eventually death.

Here we have a chance to repent, be forgiven of our sins, and learn to live righteously.

Here our spirits wait to be reunited with our body through the miracle of resurrection.

If we are righteous, we can visit other spirits here who are also waiting for the resurrection.

Here we will be brought into God's presence for a final judgment, according to our works.

Here we will remember perfectly all of our right and wrong choices. If we have repented, we will receive mercy from God.

Here those who were valiant in keeping God's commandments will be rewarded with eternal life and will live with God again.

**FEBRUARY Theme: The Earth Was Created for Heavenly Father's Children**

***PRACTICE TIME:***

**. SCRIPTURE MEMORIZATION—ABRAHAM 3:24–25** (shown left). Posters and cards are available to download from GospelGrabBag.com.

**. PRACTICE SONG—Sing "My Heavenly Father Loves Me"** (*Children's Songbook*, 228–29) using the song visuals (shown right). These are available to download from GospelGrabBag.com.

***SHARING TIME, Week 1:***
***Jesus Christ created the earth under the direction of Heavenly Father.***

***ACTIVITY: Let's Create the Creation***
***(Days 1–7 Scripture Scramble)***

**OBJECTIVE:** Help youth learn that Jesus Christ created the earth, where they could go to gain a body, grow, and learn. They can scramble, search for, and read these scriptures to learn about the creation days 1–7.

**TO MAKE:** Copy, color, and cut out the images that follow. Use tape/magnets to mount the visuals.

**ACTIVITY:**

1. Mount images on the board or around the room or one under the chairs for each youth. Ask them, "What needed to be created in order for us to gain a body so we could grow and learn?" The earth. "Who did Heavenly Father choose to create this earth?" Jesus. (Show His picture.)
2. Have children from each class take turns randomly choosing a number posted on the board or around the room. Then have them scramble to find their scriptures.
3. Post their numbers in order and read them, telling about their day of creation as follows—

**Days 1–7 Creation:** On Day 1, God created the heavens and the earth and divided light and darkness (Genesis 1:3–5); on Day 2, He divided the land and water (Genesis 1:6–10); on Day 3, He created flowers, trees, fruit, and vegetables (Genesis 1:11–13); on Day 4, He created the sun, moon, and stars (Genesis 1:14–19); on Day 5, He created land animals, water animals, and birds (Genesis 1:20–25); on Day 6, He created man (Genesis 1:26–27); and on Day 7, He rested (Genesis 2:1–3).

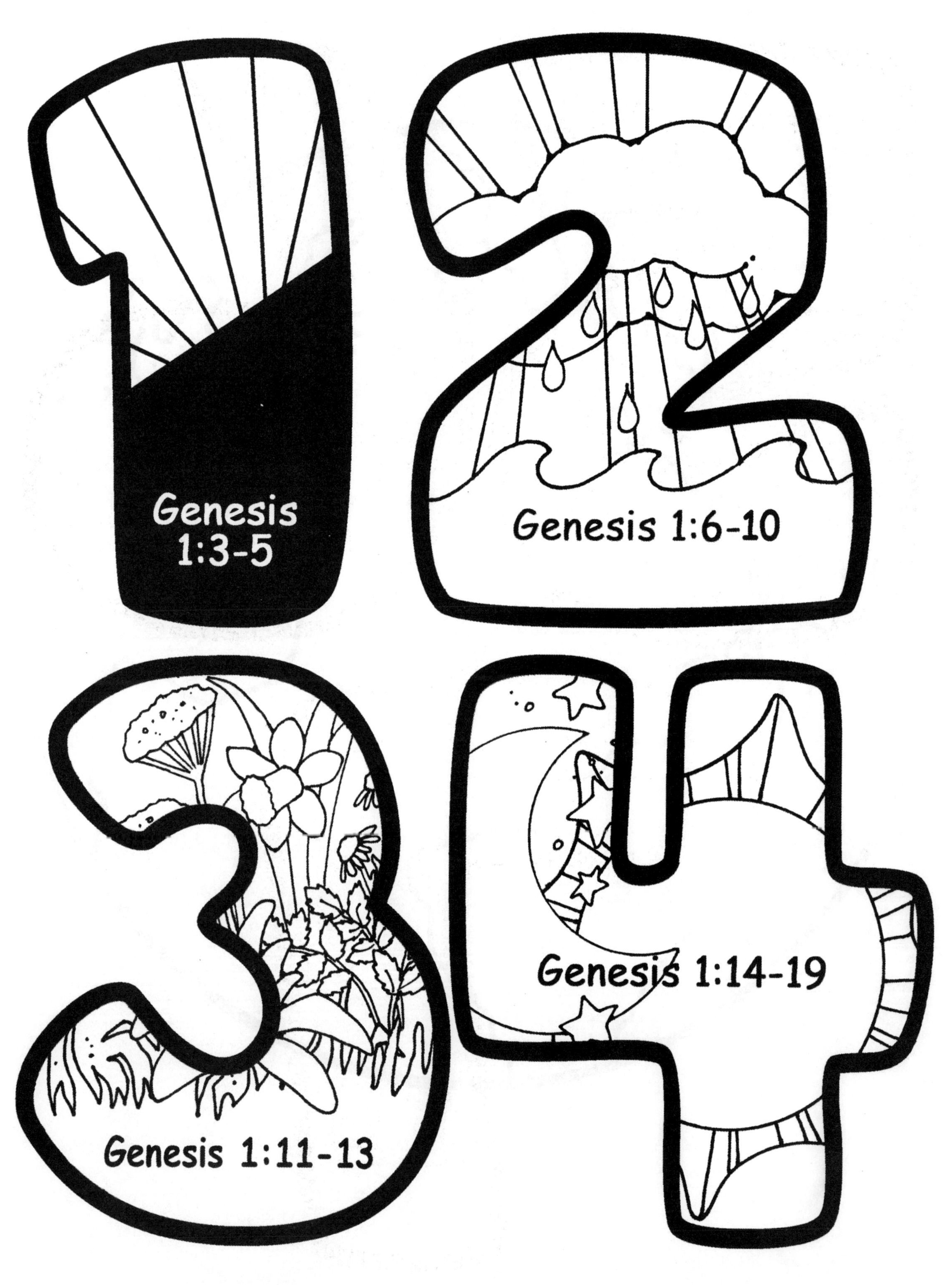
Genesis
1:3-5
Genesis 1:6-10
Genesis 1:11-13
Genesis 1:14-19

Genesis 1:20-25
Genesis 1:26-27
Genesis 2:1-3

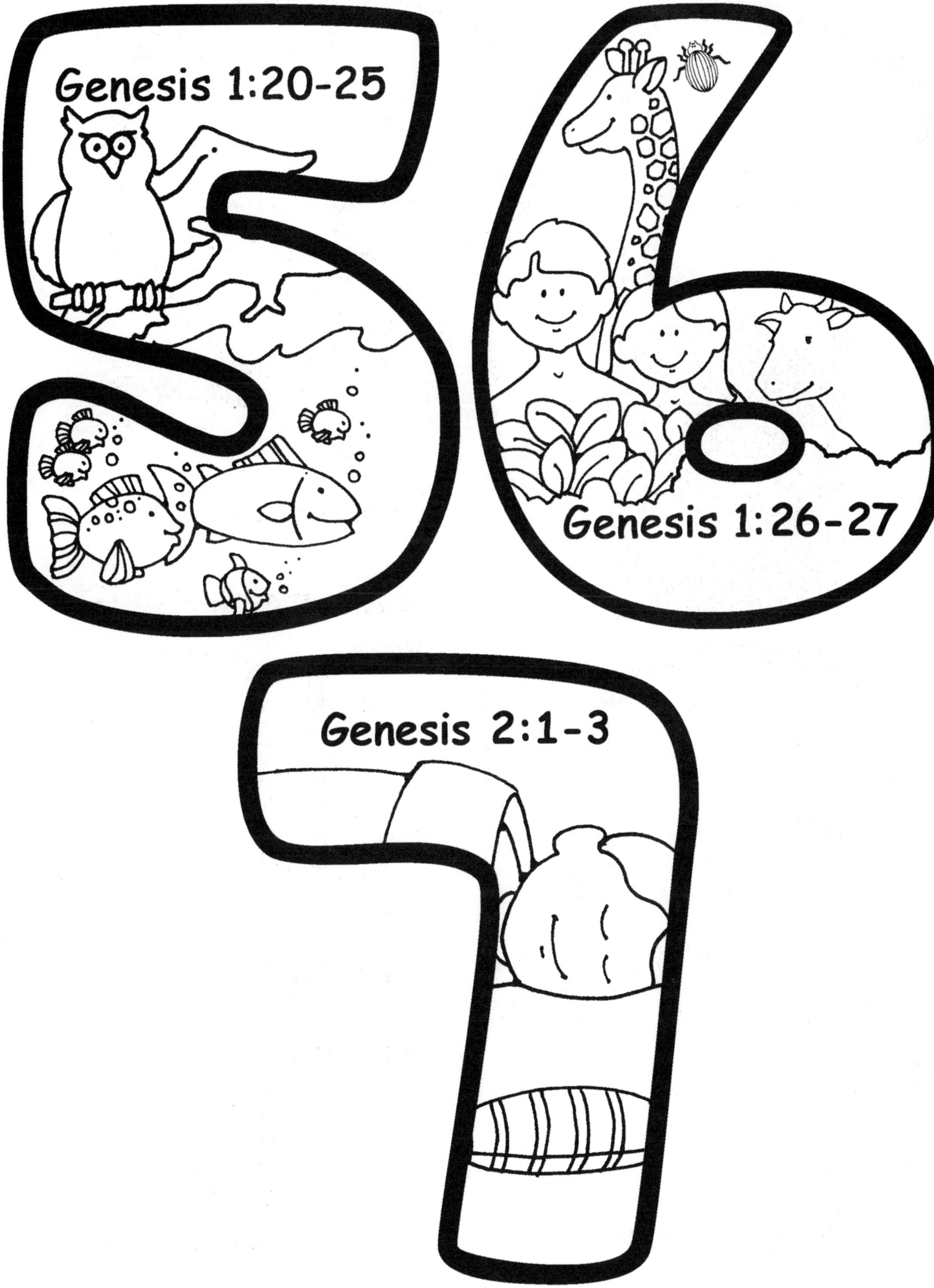

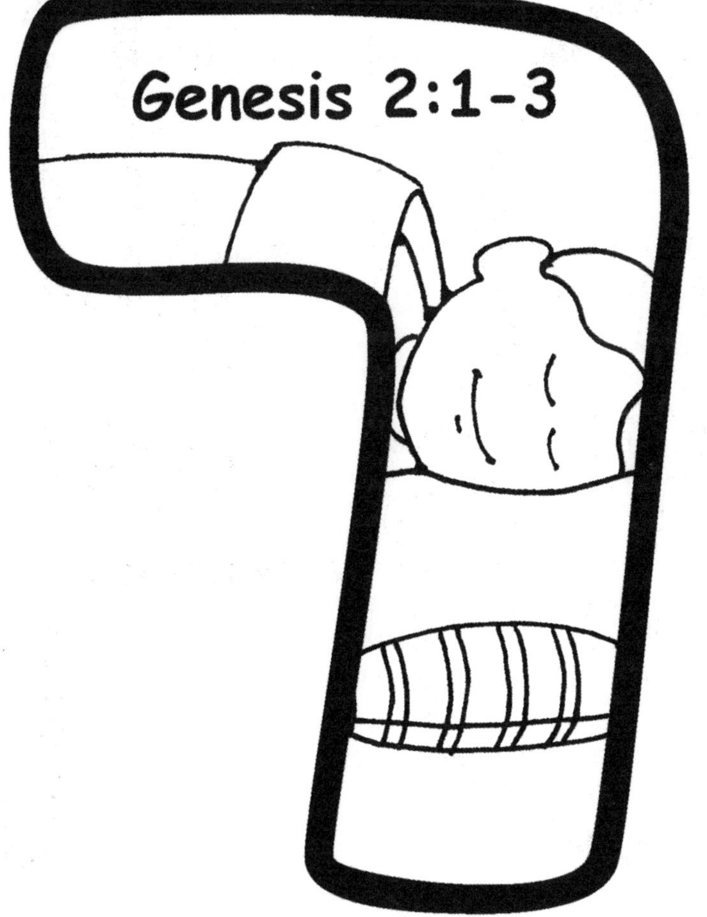

## FEBRUARY Theme: The Earth Was Created for Heavenly Father's Children

***PRACTICE TIME (download scripture & song visuals shown on p. 7 from GospelGrabBag.com)***

## *SHARING TIME, Week 4:*
## *If I keep the commandments, I can live with Heavenly Father again.*

### *ACTIVITY: Keeping Inside the Fence*
### *(Commandments Keep Us Safe Quiz)*

**OBJECTIVE:** Teach children that we can be safe from physical and spiritual dangers. As we (the sheep) keep the commandments, we can stay inside the fence (see commandments on the fence). If we do not keep the commandments, we are subject to dangers: wolves, rocks, river, pit. If we go outside the fence, we can repent and go back inside to keep safe.

**TO MAKE:** Copy, color, and cut out the images that follow. Use tape/magnets to mount the visuals.

**ACTIVITY:**

1. Mount the fence pieces on the board and the sheep around the room or under chairs. Talk about the rules we need to obey to stay safe. Parents and leaders show love when they give us these rules. Heavenly Father has given us rules called commandments, and we are His sheep. Talk about the OBJECTIVE (above). Briefly tell the parable of the sheep, where Jesus found the one that was lost (Matthew 18:12 / Luke 15:1–7).
2. Ask the children to find a sheep and read the action. If the sheep obeyed God's commandment, tell ***how it gives us safety and peace,*** then PLACE SHEEP INSIDE THE FENCE. If they did not obey, tell ***how it brings danger,*** then PLACE SHEEP OUTSIDE THE FENCE with the wolves, rocks, river, and pit.
3. If there is time, the children can find the lost sheep and tell what they could do to repent and choose the right, then PLACE THE SHEEP INSIDE THE FENCE where there is safety.

Cut carefully along inside of dotted line.

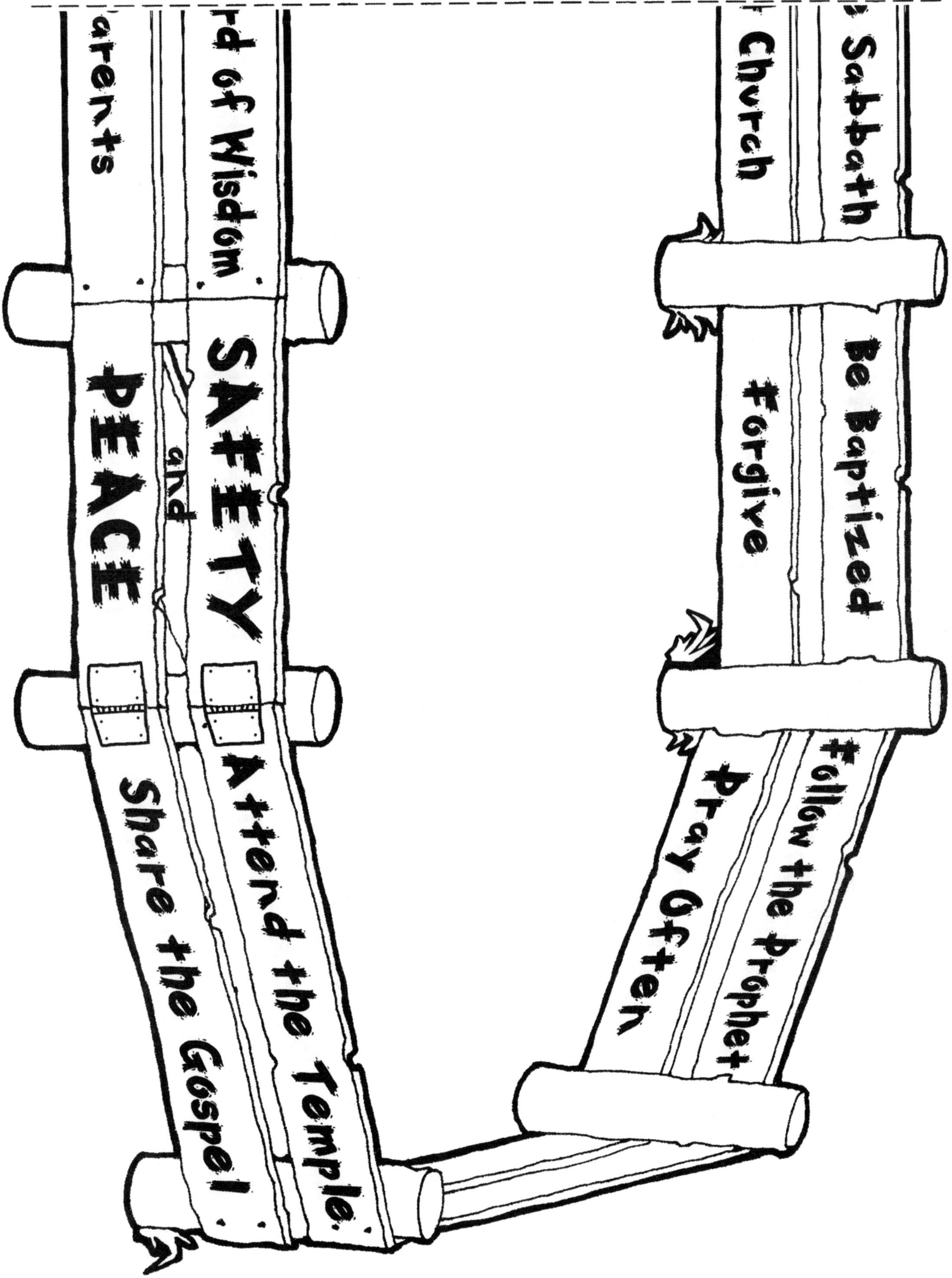

arents

rd of Wisdom

SAFETY

and

PEACE

Share the Gospel.

Attend the Temple.

Church

Sabbath

Be Baptized

Forgive

Follow the Prophet

Pray Often

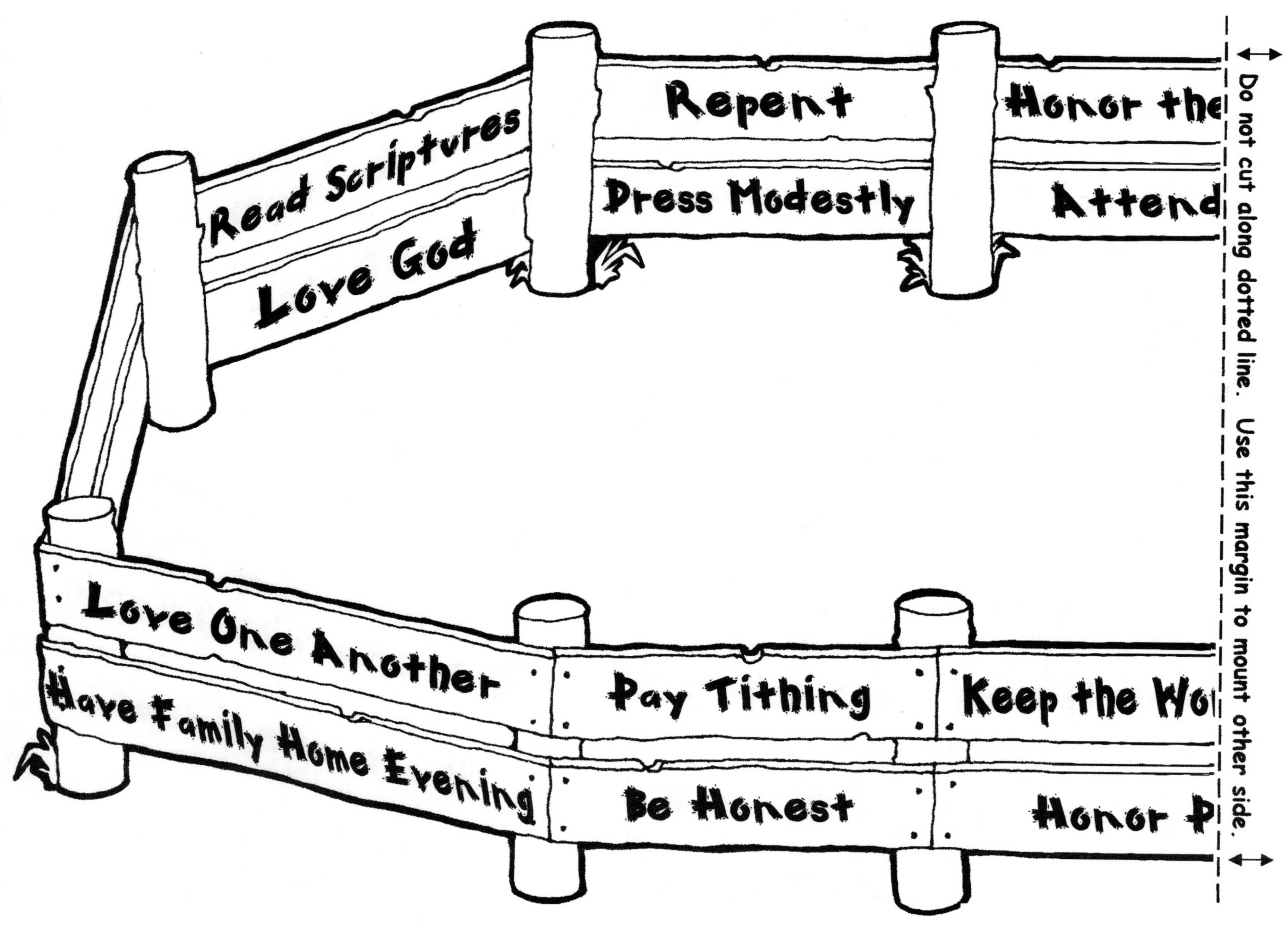


Do not cut along dotted line. Use this margin to mount other side.

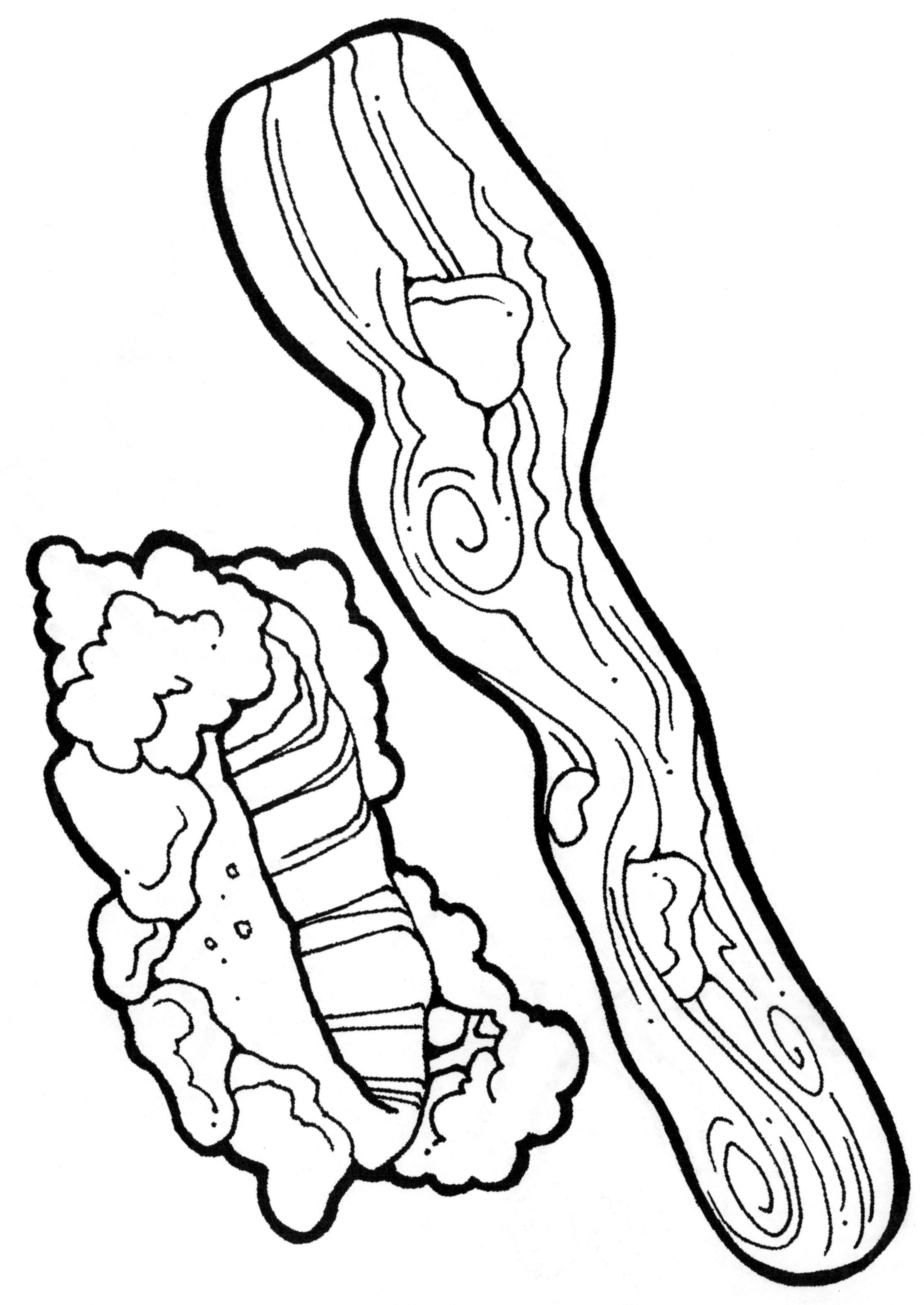

It seems okay to be unkind to a kid at school; my friends are doing it. WHAT IS THE DANGER OF THIS DECISION?
My grandmother was old, and her yard was full of weeds, so I got to work. HOW DOES THIS PROVIDE SAFETY AND PEACE?
My friend likes to wear short shorts,but I choose not to. HOW DOES THIS PROVIDE SAFETY AND PEACE?
My friend said she was sorry, but I didn't want to forgive her or talk to her. WHAT IS THE DANGER OF THIS DECISION?
Before I turned eight years old, I decided to be baptized and follow Jesus. HOW DOES THIS PROVIDE SAFETY AND PEACE?
It was Sunday, and my friends asked me to play; I said I would instead of going to church. WHAT IS THE DANGER OF THIS DECISION?
I told my mom I would call her so she could meet me, but I walked home by myself instead. WHAT IS THE DANGER OF THIS DECISION?
I am trying to live in a way that I can be sealed to my family in the temple or that when I am twelve, I can be baptized for the dead. HOW DOES THIS PROVIDE SAFETY AND PEACE?
My friend asked me about what I believe, and I was too scared to tell her. WHAT IS THE DANGER OF THIS DECISION?
When mom called for family home evening, I was cross and disagreeable.
WHAT IS THE DANGER OF THIS DECISION?

The kids in my class were talking instead of listening to the teacher, so I said, "Let's be reverent, guys." HOW DOES THIS PROVIDE SAFETY AND PEACE?
I started to think about a movie I liked during Primary but decided to listen to the teacher instead. HOW DOES THIS PROVIDE SAFETY AND PEACE?
I saw someone who needed my help, but I passed them by. WHAT IS THE DANGER OF THIS DECISION?
My friend didn't use the name of Jesus reverently, so I asked him not to swear. HOW DOES THIS PROVIDE SAFETY AND PEACE?
I heard an unclean joke that was kind of funny, but I didn't laugh or tell it to others. HOW DOES THIS PROVIDE SAFETY AND PEACE?
I was saving for a new bike and decided to spend my tithing money. WHAT IS THE DANGER OF THIS DECISION?
My friend wanted me to see bad pictures on the computer, so I left the room. HOW DOES THIS PROVIDE SAFETY AND PEACE?
My family didn't want to have scripture study, so I decided to do it on my own. HOW DOES THIS PROVIDE SAFETY AND PEACE?
When I take the sacrament, I remember the sacred promises and try to keep them during the week. HOW DOES THIS PROVIDE SAFETY AND PEACE?
I promised Mom I would be home before 6:00, but I wasn't, even though I knew what time it was.
WHAT IS THE DANGER OF THIS DECISION?

On Saturday, I helped get the work done so we could rest and worship on Sunday. HOW DOES THIS PROVIDE SAFETY AND PEACE?
My friend had a popular video game he wanted me to play, but it was violent, and I told him I wouldn't. HOW DOES THIS PROVIDE SAFETY AND PEACE?
I told my friend I was sorry when I hurt his feelings. HOW DOES THIS PROVIDE SAFETY AND PEACE?
My friend's parents let him drink coffee, and they said I could have some. I said no. HOW DOES THIS PROVIDE SAFETY AND PEACE?
My friend likes to listen to a song with bad words in it, so I listen too. WHAT IS THE DANGER OF THIS DECISION?
When I go to bed, I crash on my pillow but then remember to kneel and pray. HOW DOES THIS PROVIDE SAFETY AND PEACE?
It was time to watch conference, and I decided to listen to what the prophet said. HOW DOES THIS PROVIDE SAFETY AND PEACE?
I forgot to study for my test at school, so I let my friend give me the answers. WHAT IS THE DANGER OF THIS DECISION?
I took a piece of candy at the store and didn't tell Mom or pay for it.
WHAT IS THE DANGER OF THIS DECISION?
My friend wanted me to watch a bad movie, but I followed the prophet and said no. HOW DOES THIS PROVIDE SAFETY AND PEACE?

# MARCH Theme: Jesus Christ Is Our Savior

## *PRACTICE TIME:*

. **SCRIPTURE MEMORIZATION—D&C 43:34** (shown left). Posters and cards are available to download from GospelGrabBag.com.

. **PRACTICE SONG—Sing "If the Savior Stood Beside Me"** (*Friend,* Oct. 1993, 14) using the song visuals (shown right). These are available to download from GospelGrabBag.com.

## *SHARING TIME, Week 1:* *Because Jesus Christ was resurrected, I will be too.*

## *ACTIVITY: Resurrection Miracles (Match Game)*

**OBJECTIVE:** Children will learn about the miracle of the Resurrection with this Resurrection Miracles—Match Game. They will learn that through His Resurrection, Jesus made it possible for us to be resurrected and receive a perfect body. (See D&C 138:14.)

**TO MAKE:** Copy, color, and cut out the images that follow. Use tape/magnets to mount the visuals. Laminate and cut out.

**ACTIVITY:**

1. Talk to children about the Resurrection of Jesus, and tell them that because of Jesus's Resurrection, we will all receive a perfect body. Sometimes in this life, we suffer physical difficulties, but through Christ's Resurrection, everything about our bodies will be restored to their perfect form when we are resurrected. Read and talk about:

• Alma 40:23: "The soul shall be restored to the body, and the body to the soul; yea, and every limb and joint shall be restored to its body; yea, even a hair of the head shall not be lost; but all things shall be restored to their proper and perfect frame."

• D&C 9:14: "Stand fast in the work wherewith I have called you, and a hair of your head shall not be lost, and you shall be lifted up at the last day."

2. Tell children they are going to learn about those who have lived on the earth and passed on. They are now in the grave, but we have hope that, because of Jesus's Resurrection, they will live again. Read D&C 138:14: "All these had departed the mortal life, firm in the hope of a glorious resurrection, through the grace of God the Father and his Only Begotten Son, Jesus Christ."

3. Mount the match cards on the board with the first part of the card/story on the left and the second part of the card/story on the right. Have children take turns finding matching cards by matching up the body part and reading the story. Two children can team up and do this, each one reading their part of the card (with the child who retrieved the card on the left of the board reading his first).

4. Talk about each situation and how nice it will be when we can all be resurrected. If there is time, have children share stories of loved ones who have passed and why they will be happy when they are resurrected.

19–29 (Instructions & Visuals)

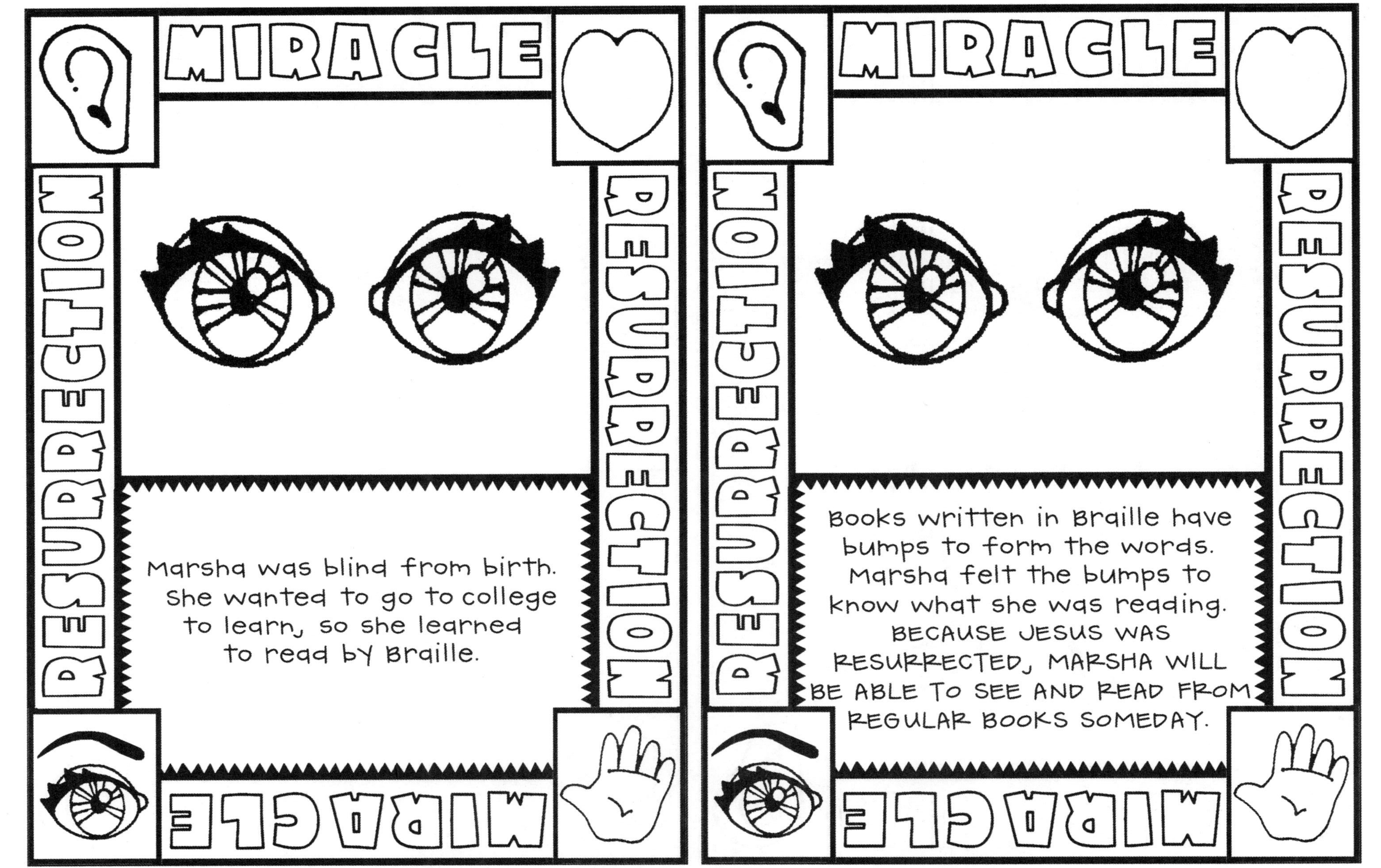
MIRACLE
RESURRECTION
Marsha was blind from birth. She wanted to go to college to learn, so she learned to read by Braille.
MIRACLE
RESURRECTION
Books written in Braille have bumps to form the words. Marsha felt the bumps to know what she was reading. BECAUSE JESUS WAS RESURRECTED, MARSHA WILL BE ABLE TO SEE AND READ FROM REGULAR BOOKS SOMEDAY.

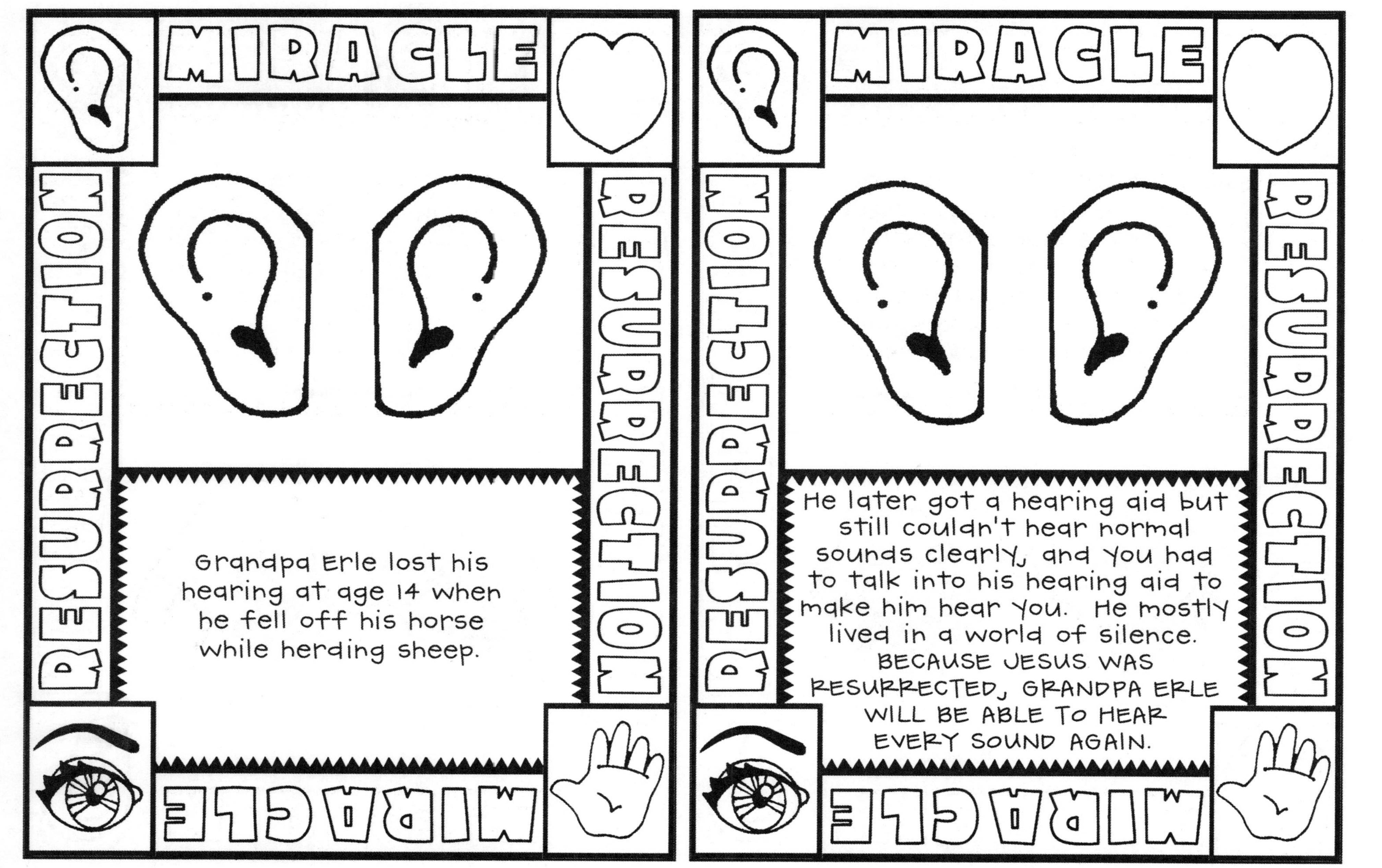
MIRACLE
RESURRECTION
RESURRECTION
MIRACLE
Grandpa Erle lost his hearing at age 14 when he fell off his horse while herding sheep.
MIRACLE
RESURRECTION
RESURRECTION
MIRACLE
He later got a hearing aid but still couldn't hear normal sounds clearly, and you had to talk into his hearing aid to make him hear you. He mostly lived in a world of silence.
BECAUSE JESUS WAS RESURRECTED, GRANDPA ERLE WILL BE ABLE TO HEAR EVERY SOUND AGAIN.

MIRACLE
RESURRECTION
RESURRECTION
Glen was always thankful for his body because he was born without his right hand. Even though Glen had difficulty doing things, he always tried to do the best he could.
MIRACLE
MIRACLE
RESURRECTION
RESURRECTION
On the family farm, he picked fruit with his one good hand. He also helped lift baskets of fruit onto the wagons going to market. BECAUSE JESUS WAS RESURRECTED, GLEN WILL RECEIVE THE HAND HE NEVER HAD.
MIRACLE

MIRACLE
RESURRECTION
RESURRECTION
Steve was so happy to get braces to straighten his pearly white teeth. He kept brushing and flossing them faithfully every day. When his braces came off, his teeth were straight and beautiful.
MIRACLE
MIRACLE
RESURRECTION
RESURRECTION
Many months later, Steve went swimming and dove into the pool and hit his two front teeth on the bottom, breaking them off. The dentist put caps to cover the broken parts, but they weren't his real teeth.
BECAUSE JESUS WAS RESURRECTED, STEVE WILL HAVE HIS PEARLY WHITES AGAIN.
MIRACLE

MIRACLE
RESURRECTION
RESURRECTION
Uncle Lucas was the fastest runner in his school and won first place on his track team two years in a row. When he was 19, he went to war and fought bravely.
MIRACLE
MIRACLE
RESURRECTION
RESURRECTION
Because a bomb hit their camp, he lost his leg and had to wear an artificial leg the rest of his life. He was not able to run anymore and had a slight limp.
BECAUSE JESUS WAS RESURRECTED, UNCLE LUCAS WILL BE ABLE TO RUN AGAIN.
MIRACLE

MIRACLE
RESURRECTION
RESURRECTION
Grandpa Hatch was the kids' favorite grandpa. He used to play checkers and other games with them. He would talk to them about their troubles, and he knew just what to say.
MIRACLE
MIRACLE
RESURRECTION
RESURRECTION
One day, Grandpa got really sick with pneumonia. He lay in bed for a long time, got weaker and weaker, and finally died.
BECAUSE JESUS WAS RESURRECTED, THE CHILDREN WILL BE ABLE TO BE WITH THEIR GRANDPA AGAIN.
MIRACLE

MIRACLE
RESURRECTION
RESURRECTION
When Gladys was a little girl, she liked to dance. But one day, she got sick with rheumatic fever, and the illness damaged her heart.
MIRACLE
MIRACLE
RESURRECTION
RESURRECTION
Because her heart could not be repaired, her heart got weaker, so she had to be in bed most of the time.
BECAUSE JESUS WAS RESURRECTED, GLADYS WILL RECEIVE A NEW HEART AND DANCE ONCE AGAIN.
MIRACLE

MIRACLE
RESURRECTION
A mother gave birth to a baby too early, and the baby's lungs were not strong enough, so the baby couldn't breathe.
MIRACLE
RESURRECTION
The day the baby was born, she died. The parents were very sad and prayed that they would be able to raise their baby girl someday.
BECAUSE JESUS WAS RESURRECTED, THE BABY WILL LIVE AGAIN AND HAVE A STRONG, PERFECT BODY.

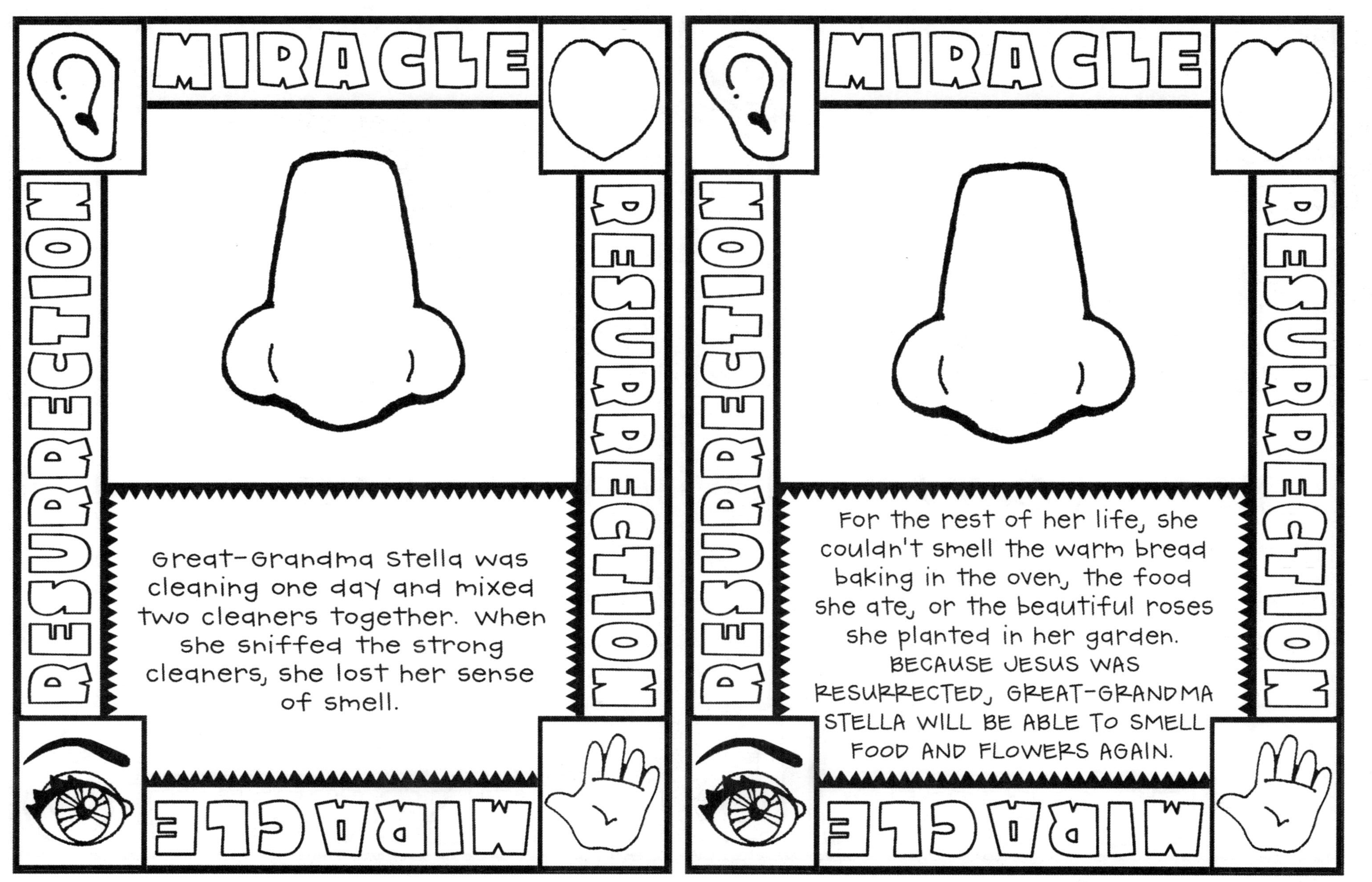
MIRACLE
RESURRECTION
RESURRECTION
Great-Grandma Stella was cleaning one day and mixed two cleaners together. When she sniffed the strong cleaners, she lost her sense of smell.
MIRACLE
MIRACLE
RESURRECTION
RESURRECTION
For the rest of her life, she couldn't smell the warm bread baking in the oven, the food she ate, or the beautiful roses she planted in her garden.
BECAUSE JESUS WAS RESURRECTED, GREAT-GRANDMA STELLA WILL BE ABLE TO SMELL FOOD AND FLOWERS AGAIN.
MIRACLE

MIRACLE
RESURRECTION
RESURRECTION
Otto was a good-looking young man, everyone said. People would stop and tell him he had a nice face.
MIRACLE
MIRACLE
RESURRECTION
RESURRECTION
One day, Otto got in a car accident, and the car caught fire. Otto's face was badly burned and scarred. He had plastic surgery to make it look better, but he wasn't the same.
BECAUSE JESUS WAS RESURRECTED, OTTO WILL HAVE HIS HANDSOME FACE AGAIN.
MIRACLE

## MARCH Theme: Jesus Christ Is Our Savior

***PRACTICE TIME (see scripture memorization and singing time ideas, p. 19):***

### *SHARING TIME, Week 4:*
### *Jesus Christ Is Our Savior.*

### *ACTIVITY: Guess Who Was Saved by the Savior*
### *(Forgiveness Scripture Stories)*

**OBJECTIVE:** Help children learn many stories of those who were blessed by the Atonement. Because Jesus suffered for us in the Garden of Gethsemane and died for us, we will be saved like these people.

**TO MAKE:** Copy, color, and cut out the images that follow. Make three copies of the smiley faces. Mount the word strips on the backs of the faces. Laminate. Use tape or magnets to mount visuals. Mount stories on the backs of the faces.

**ACTIVITY:**

1. Tell children/youth that Jesus is a life saver just like someone who would save our life today, like a policeman, a doctor, or a lifeguard. Only Jesus saves us from sin and death. He suffered and died for us so we can repent if we do wrong and make our life different. We can choose the right and find peace and happiness. Jesus saved us from sin so we can return to live again with Him and with Heavenly Father. If we repent and keep His commandments, we can feel safe and happy.

2. Have children/youth take turns choosing a face, with the story found on the back, to read about that someone who was saved by Jesus. At the end of the story, say, "Guess who was saved by the Savior?" and then have children/youth guess who it was. The ones reading the stories can listen to the others' guesses. When the right one is said, they can post the picture on the board. Or they can tell who it was if the name was not guessed.

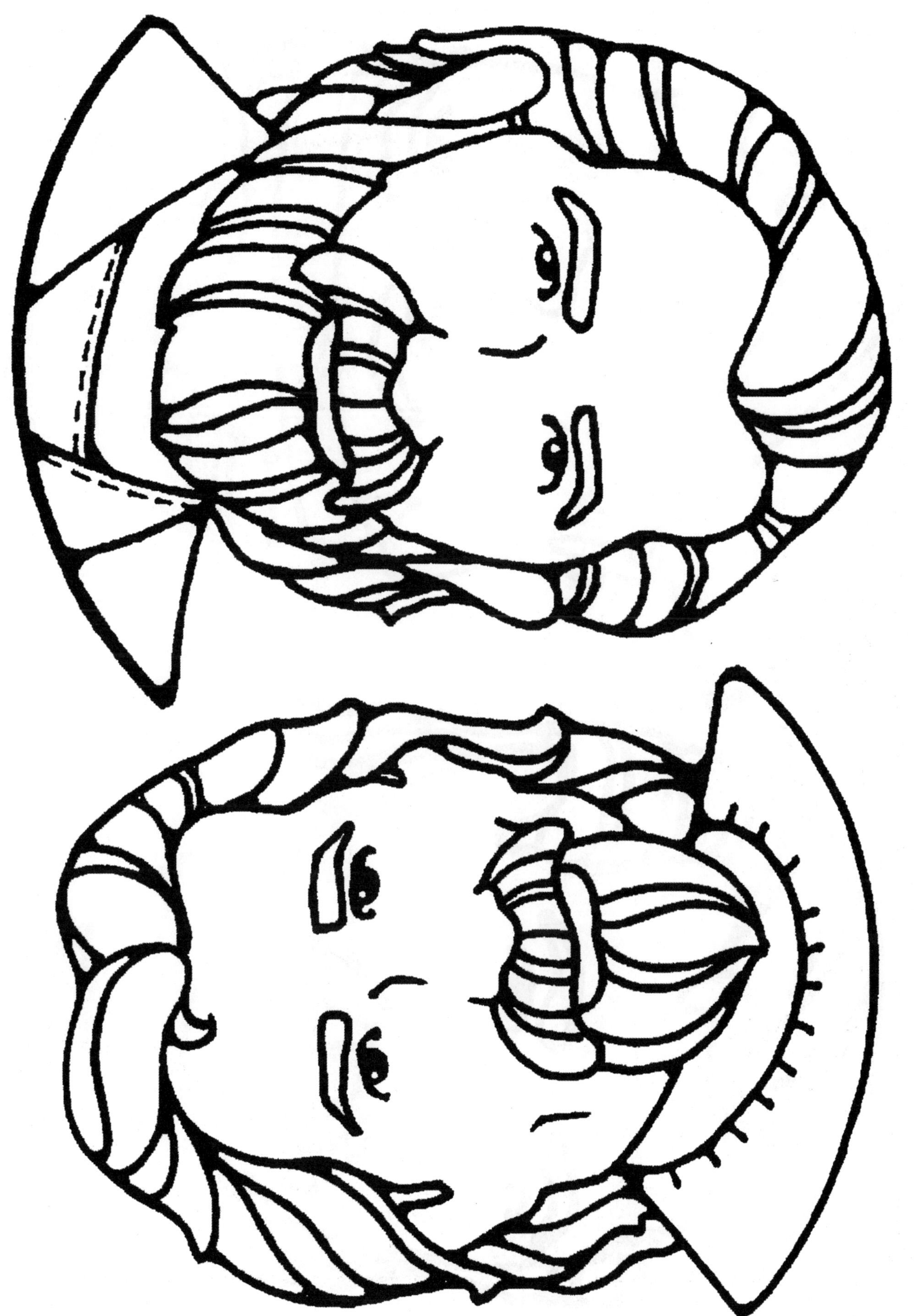

Alma the Younger

Enos

Zeezrom

Lamoni's Father

Man brought to Jesus

Jesus Christ
Cut carefully along
inside of dotted line.
Do not cut along dotted line.
Use this to mount other side.
is Our Savior

STORIES TO PLACE ON BACKS OF FACES:

I went about with my friends, the sons of Mosiah, trying to destroy the Church of God. I fell to the earth with fear as an angel came, telling me I would be destroyed if I didn't stop seeking to destroy God's Church.

I could not speak or move my limbs for three days. I was tormented with my sins because I had rebelled against God. I was horrified to meet God. I remembered what my father, the prophet, said about the coming of Jesus Christ, the Son of God, to atone for the sins of the world. I cried for Jesus to have mercy on me, and by doing this, the horror of my sins left me, my soul was filled with light, and I felt sweet joy. I went out to bring souls to repentance. ALMA THE YOUNGER (Alma 36:6–24)

I knew my father was a just man, for he taught me the things of God. I went to hunt beasts in the forest, and there I remembered my father's words about eternal life and the joy of the Saints. These sank deep into my heart. My soul hungered for these truths as I knelt and cried in mighty prayer. I prayed all day and night, hoping my prayers would reach heaven. There came a voice, saying that my sins were forgiven and I would be blessed. I knew God would not lie, and my guilt was swept away. The Lord said He did it because of my faith in Him. He said my faith would make me whole and happy again. ENOS (Enos 1:1–8)

I lay sick with a burning fever as I remembered the wicked things I had done. I thought Alma and Amulek were dead because of me, and I sorrowed, without hope that I would be happy again. But hearing they were still alive, I took courage and sent a message for them to come to me. Seeing them, I stretched forth my hand for them to heal me. Taking me by the hand, they asked, "Believest thou in the power of Christ unto salvation?" I said I believed all the words they taught. Alma said if I believed in the redemption of Christ, I could be healed. I said I believed, and he asked God to have mercy on me and heal me because of my faith. I leaped to my feet and began to walk. I was then baptized and began to preach unto the people. ZEEZROM (Alma 15:3–12)

Aaron, the brother of Ammon, came to the land of Nephi, saying he would be my servant. I was the king over all the Lamanites. He told me about God and that He is the Great Spirit who brought our fathers out of the land of Jerusalem. He said I must believe and repent or I would be cast off in the last day. Aaron said this God created all things. I bowed down before God and repented of all my sins so I would receive hope that there was a God. I said I would give away all of my sins to know this, be raised from the dead, and be saved in the last day. After I said this, I was struck as if I were dead. Then I was raised up again to life. I told my people to believe and listen to Aaron and his brethren.
LAMONI'S FATHER (Alma 22:1–26)

During the time Jesus lived in Jerusalem, I was taken with palsy and could not walk. People tried to get me to Jesus, but there were so many people, they could not. So they took me on my couch upon the housetop and let me down through the house where Jesus was. When Jesus saw the faith of my friends, He said to me, "Man, thy sins are forgiven thee. . . . Rise up and take up thy couch and go into thine house." I walked again and glorified God.
MAN BROUGHT TO JESUS (Luke 5:17–26)

## APRIL Theme: Jesus Christ Restored His Church in the Latter Days

### *PRACTICE TIME:*

. **MEMORIZE—D&C 35:17** (shown left). Posters and cards are available to download from GospelGrabBag.com.
. **PRACTICE SONG "An Angel Came to Joseph Smith"** (*Hymns*, 239) using the song visuals (shown right). These are available to download from GospelGrabBag.com.

### *SHARING TIME, Week 1:* *After Jesus Christ and His Apostles died, gospel truths were lost.*

### *ACTIVITY: Restored Truths (Lost-and-Found Gospel Treasures)*

**OBJECTIVE:** Help children learn about the gospel treasures Jesus brought to the earth. They will learn how the gospel treasures were lost when Jesus died and how they were found again when Joseph Smith restored the true gospel of Jesus Christ to the earth.

**TO MAKE:** Copy, color, and cut out the images that follow. Cut out the treasure box and both sets of treasures and instructions and clues. Laminate. Mount treasure chest on a poster. Using an Exacto knife, cut along the dotted lines on the inside of the chest and treasure mounds to later insert jewels.

**ACTIVITY:** (Choose from two options)
***Option 1:***

1. Talk about Jesus Christ organizing His Church on the earth and bringing to the earth gospel treasures *(the first set of **jewels**)*: PROPHETS, BAPTISM, HOLY GHOST, COMMANDMENTS, MISSIONARIES, SCRIPTURES, PRIESTHOOD, TEMPLES, and SACRAMENT. As children place each jewel in the treasure box, talk about each and why Jesus wanted each to organize His Church.
2. Talk about the Apostasy and how these gospel treasures were taken from the earth *(the second set of **jewels**)*. Have children help you take the jewels out of the treasure chest as you talk about each.
3. Talk about the Restoration (see *Ideas* below), and have children help you place the second set of jewels in the chest, bringing back the gospel treasures (different modern-day images but the same gospel treasures that were here when Jesus was upon the earth).

***Option 2:*** This is more appealing to older children (copy and cut out the clue cards if using this option). Follow steps #1–3 above but have children guess each gospel treasure using the clues on the clue cards. Have children draw a clue card and hand it to the leader to read. You can have them play in teams to compete and take turns guessing which gospel treasures the clues are about. Whoever guesses the gospel treasure correctly can find the jewel and place it in the treasure chest.

**Ideas to Present Treasure Chest: Jesus Christ Organized His Church.** Say the following and place the "organization" (first set of jewels) in the treasure chest (as follows).

**PROPHETS:** Before Jesus came, the world was created and many people lived on the earth. Jesus sent prophets to teach the people about Him and to be righteous and to obey Heavenly Father's commandments. Prophets from the Old Testament told of Jesus's coming. These prophets were Adam, Noah, Abraham, Moses, and others. Also, prophets from the Book of Mormon told of His coming.

**BAPTISM:** When Jesus grew to be a man, He asked John the Baptist to baptize Him to show us it is important for everyone to be baptized and receive the Holy Ghost. Jesus organized His Church, the only true church on the earth, and chose twelve Apostles to help Him teach His gospel.

**COMMANDMENTS:** When Jesus was on the earth, He taught the people the Ten Commandments given to Moses and gave them many other commandments to follow so they could be happy.

**MISSIONARIES:** When Jesus called His twelve Apostles, they became missionaries who went out to preach the gospel of Jesus Christ. They taught the people about Heavenly Father's plan of salvation. They were called fishers of men.

**SCRIPTURES:** Jesus and His Apostles taught from the scriptures. The writings, or true stories about Jesus, also became scripture. The New Testament tells about Jesus's life on earth. The Book of Mormon also tells about Jesus visiting the earth.

**PRIESTHOOD:** Jesus gave His Apostles the priesthood, which is a special power from Heavenly Father. With this priesthood, Jesus and His Apostles were able to perform miracles, heal the sick, bless the downtrodden, and perform baptisms and temple ordinances.

**TEMPLES:** Before Jesus came to the earth, prophets guided people to build temples. As a boy, Jesus was found teaching the priests in the temple and answering their questions about Heavenly Father's plan.

**SACRAMENT:** Jesus gave His Apostles the sacrament. He blessed bread and water and gave it to them, telling them to remember His sacrifice of giving His life for us and to always remember to keep the commandments.

Cut carefully along the inside of the dotted line.

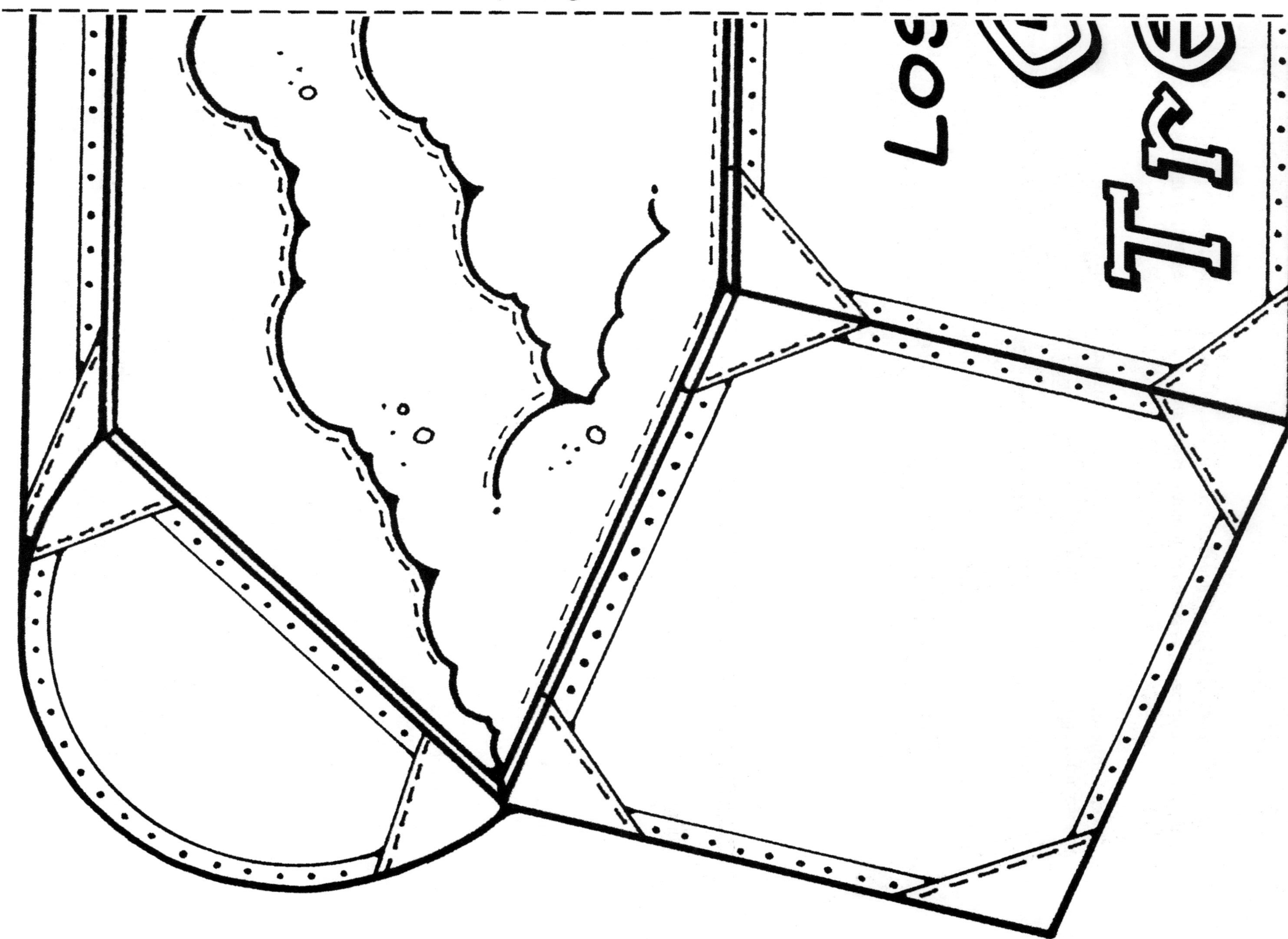

Do not cut along the dotted line. Use this margin to mount the other side.

Prophets #1
Holy Ghost #1
Baptism #1

Scriptures #1
Priesthood #1
Commandments #1
Missionaries #1

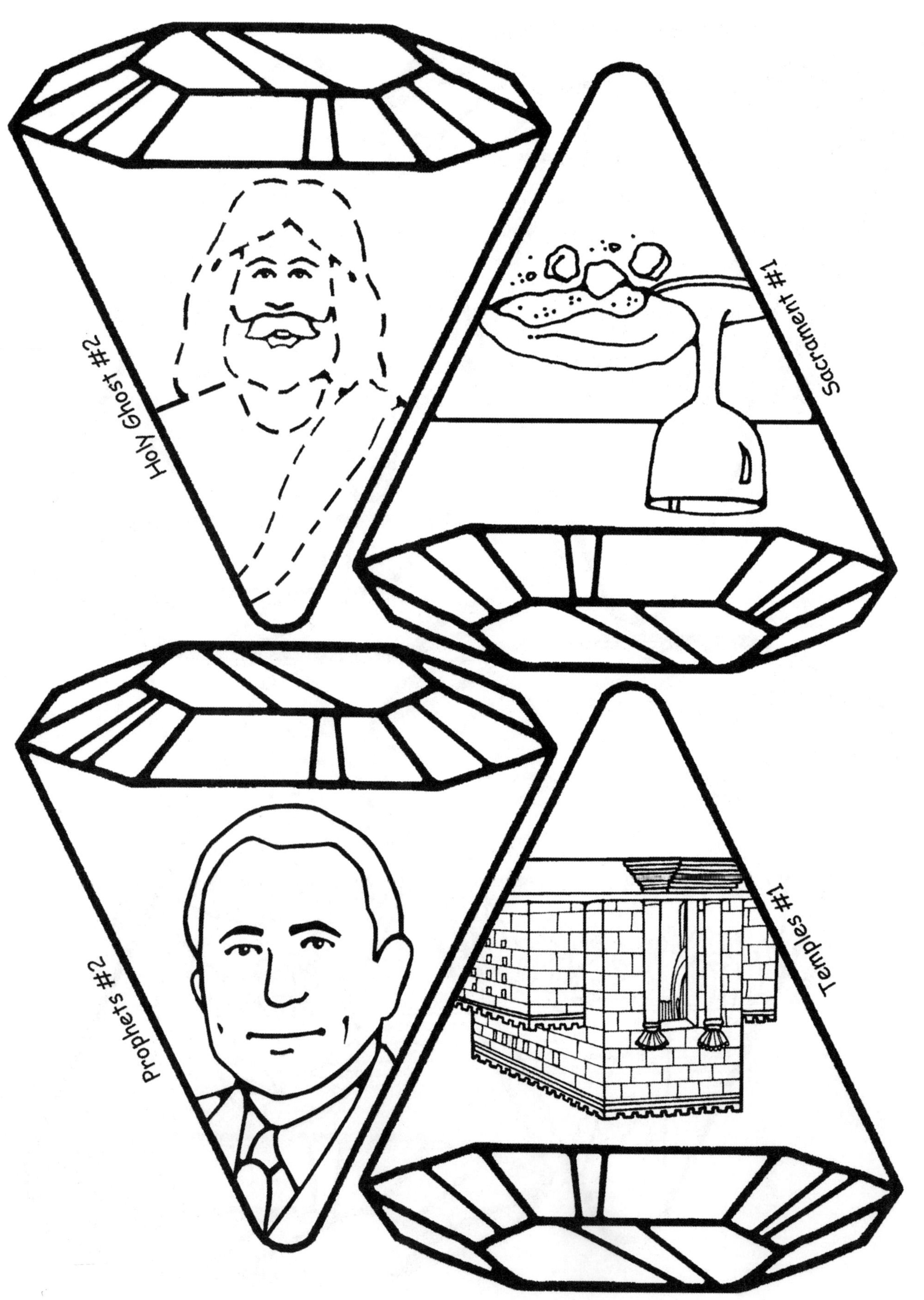

Holy Ghost #2
Sacrament #1
Prophets #2
Temples #1

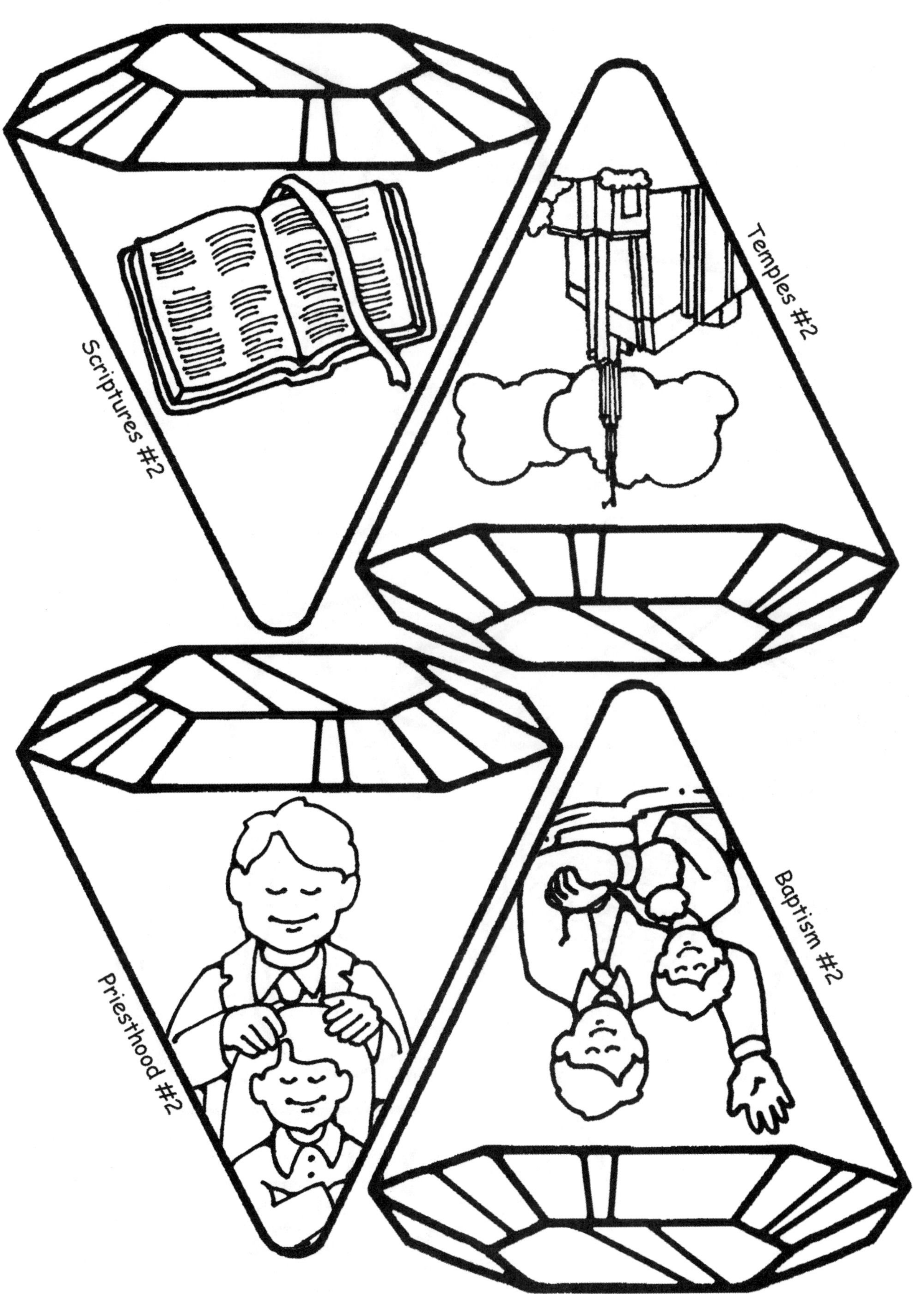

Scriptures #2
Temples #2
Priesthood #2
Baptism #2

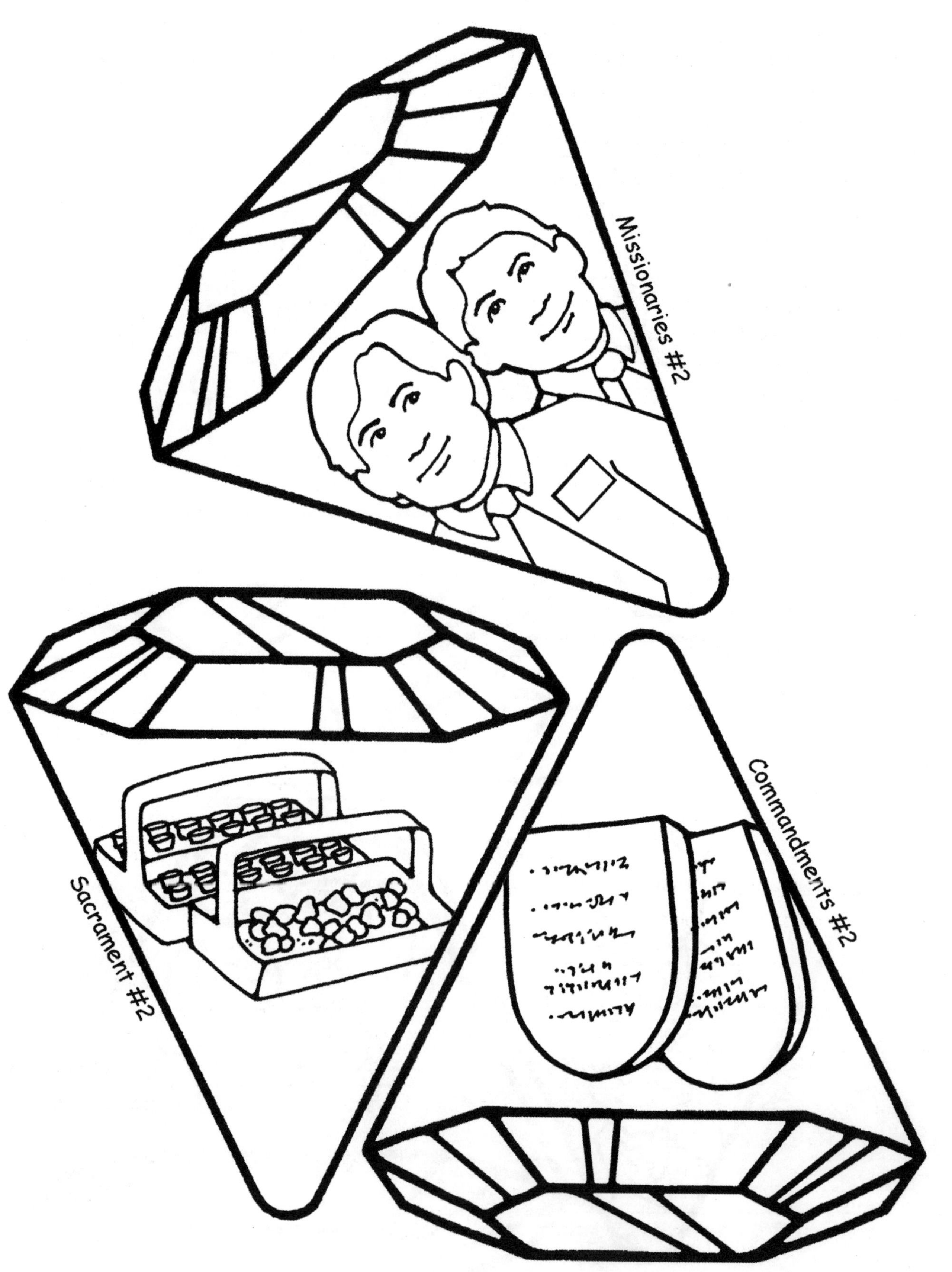
Missionaries #2
Sacrament #2
Commandments #2

### *The Apostasy—*

Say the following, and take the first set of jewels out of the treasure chest: "After Jesus died, was resurrected, and ascended to heaven, His Apostles tried to teach the gospel and hold His Church together, but many of the Apostles were also killed. Then the people started changing the teachings of Jesus and the true gospel He brought from Heavenly Father.

- **PROPHETS** and the **PRIESTHOOD** were taken off the earth.
- Some of the **SCRIPTURES** were changed.
- The **TEMPLES** were no longer built or used correctly.
- There were no longer **BAPTISMS** into Jesus Christ's true Church.
- People could no longer receive the gift of the **HOLY GHOST**.
- **MISSIONARIES** were not called to preach the gospel of Jesus Christ.
- Some **COMMANDMENTS** were taught, but many of the correct teachings were lost.
- The correct **SACRAMENTAL** ordinance was lost.

After all of these were taken away, men were left to themselves."

### *The Restoration—*

Say the following, and place the "Restoration" (second set of jewels) in the treasure chest. "Hundreds of years after Jesus's death and the beginning of the Apostasy, the people of the world were still spiritually lost. When Joseph Smith prayed as a boy of fourteen, Heavenly Father and Jesus appeared to Him and told Him that none of the churches was true. Joseph was asked to restore the true Church of Jesus Christ to the earth. These are some of the gospel treasures he restored that are on the earth today: PROPHETS, BAPTISM, COMMANDMENTS, MISSIONARIES, SCRIPTURE, PRIESTHOOD, TEMPLES, SACRAMENT."

| | |
|---|---|
| Clue 1: ancient records<br>Clue 2: found hidden in a hill<br>Clue 3: plates translated<br>SCRIPTURES (Book of Mormon) | Clue 1: Jesus used these to teach the gospel<br>Clue 2: they help you obey<br>Clue 3: avoid temptation<br>COMMANDMENTS |
| Clue 1: foreordained before the world began<br>Clue 2: mouthpiece of the Lord<br>Clue 3: prepared the way for the Savior<br>PROPHETS | Clue 1: you shall not defile or harm it<br>Clue 2: Lord dwells here<br>Clue 3: over 150 of these are built<br>TEMPLES |
| Clue 1: righteous power<br>Clue 2: bearers to be ordained<br>Clue 3: power given by God<br>PRIESTHOOD | Clue 1: only worthy members can partake<br>Clue 2: given at the Last Supper<br>Clue 3: done to remember Jesus<br>SACRAMENT |
| Clue 1: all must have this done<br>Clue 2: cleanses you from sin<br>Clue 3: must be done by immersion<br>BAPTISM | Clue 1: Jesus called them "fishers of men"<br>Clue 2: teacher of the gospel<br>Clue 3: leave home for two years<br>MISSIONARIES |
| Clue 1: received by the laying on of hands<br>Clue 2: a comforter<br>Clue 3: given after baptism<br>HOLY GHOST | |

## MAY Theme: Prophets Teach Us to Live the Restored Gospel

### *PRACTICE TIME:*

. **SCRIPTURE MEMORIZATION—Amos 3:7** (shown left). Posters and cards are available to download from GospelGrabBag.com.
. **PRACTICE SONG—Sing "We Thank Thee, Oh God, for a Prophet"** (*Hymns*, 19) using the song visuals (shown right). These are available to download from GospelGrabBag.com.

### *SHARING TIME, Weeks 1–2:*
### *The living prophet leads the Church under the direction of Jesus Christ.*

### *ACTIVITY: The Prophet is Our Coach (Heavenly Home-Run Baseball)*

**OBJECTIVE:** Learn to listen to the prophet as he coaches us through life's trials, teaching us what we must do to live with God again. Help children think carefully about their choices as they learn skills from the prophet to win at the game of life. More ideas found in this activity.

**TO MAKE:** Copy, color, and cut out the images that follow. Make two sets of the "OUT" balls page (to make ten). Laminate. On a green poster, draw a baseline two inches from border with a heavy marker (as shown). Laminate the entire poster. With tape, mount base plates on the poster. Fold and glue together dice.

**ACTIVITY:** Introduce activity as follows.

1. Tell children that playing a good game of sports requires learning skills to play the game well. When you play baseball, you have to hit the ball to get to first base. If you get three strikes, you're out.

2. To win the game of life, Heavenly Father has sent us the prophet as our coach. The more we listen to the prophet and the harder we try, the better we will play the game of life. Getting back to heaven requires that we make the right moves and play well. For example, if we don't make an effort to do as the prophet has said, we will hit a foul ball. But if we try hard, we might make a base hit, or if we go the extra mile, we can make a home run! Heavenly Father has promised us that the prophet will teach us the right moves in life and that we can trust the prophet to coach us back to our heavenly home.

**HEAVENLY HOME-RUN GAME:**

1. Divide into two teams, writing a name for each team on the chalkboard (e.g., the DANGER DODGERS and HIGH FLIERS). See 4A and 4B below to score.

2. Teams take turns playing an inning until they make three strikeouts (see 3B and 4D below). The competing team is reverent until it is their inning to play.

3. Team members take turns at bat. The leader pitches the ball to the batter by drawing a ball from the pile and reading it aloud.

(A) If the card contains words from the prophet, the leader says, "The prophet coaches us to" (then read words [e.g., "PLANT A GARDEN"]). See #4 to read the rest of the card.

(B) If the card reads "OUT! Take one ball off a base," the player didn't listen to the prophet and strikes out. The player removes a ball from a base (if one is on).

4. Then the player at bat rolls the die (to hit the ball) to see where the ball goes.

(A) If the die reads "HOME RUN!," the player moves his or her baseball around the bases to home plate to receive 4 points for his or her team. The leader then reads the HOME RUN action on the ball that tells how they played the game (e.g., "You liked to dig deep for weeds and watered every day," showing an extra-mile action to follow the prophet).

(B) If the die reads "BASE HIT!," the player moves his baseball around the field, according to the next base starting with 1st. Then the leader reads the BASE HIT action on the ball (e.g., "You pulled only the big weeds and watered only when Dad told you to," showing only a fair effort to follow the prophet). Once a player returns home, they score 4 points.

(C) If the die reads "FOUL BALL," the player gets to bat again. But first the leader reads the FOUL BALL action on the card (e.g., "You liked to drop the seeds in but hated to weed and water," showing no effort to follow the prophet). If the player rolls "FOUL BALL" again, his or her turn ends.

(D) If the die rolls "STRUCK OUT!," the player strikes out.

5. Continue playing until time is up, then add the points to determine the winning team.

### PLANT A GARDEN

**Foul Ball:** You liked to drop the seeds in but hated to weed and water.

**Base Hit:** You pulled only the big weeds and watered only when Dad told you to.

**Home Run:** You liked to dig for weeds and watered every day.

### STUDY THE SCRIPTURES

**Foul Ball:** You only read the scriptures when asked to in family home evening and Primary.

**Base Hit:** You read the scriptures on your own, even if just a few verses, once or twice a week.

**Home Run:** You read and prayed about the Book of Mormon each day.

### SHARE THE GOSPEL

**Foul Ball:** You liked to learn about the gospel but were afraid to share it.

**Base Hit:** You were ready to share the gospel but waited for others to ask.

**Home Run:** Like Ammon, you talked to your friends about your beliefs and asked them about theirs.

### FORGIVE ONE ANOTHER

**Foul Ball:** You stopped being a friend to someone who hurt your feelings.

**Base Hit:** You were slow to forgive others.

**Home Run:** You followed Jesus by forgiving everyone and telling them so.

### HAVE FAMILY HOME EVENING

**Foul Ball:** You went to family home evening only when your friends couldn't play.

**Base Hit:** You liked to go to family home evening.

**Home Run:** You loved going to family home evening and asked to give the lesson and scripture.

**REPENT**

**Foul Ball:** You didn't say you were sorry until you were caught.

**Base Hit:** Your mother asked you to apologize, and you felt better when you said you were sorry.

**Home Run:** You made an effort to say you were sorry and to right the wrong.

**KEEP THE WORD OF WISDOM**

**Foul Ball:** You said no to smoking, drinking, and drugs but yes to caffeine drinks.

**Base Hit:** You tried to eat healthy but still loved junk food.

**Home Run:** You exercised, ate right, and avoided all harmful things.

**ATTEND CHURCH MEETINGS**

**Foul Ball:** You went to some of your Sunday meetings.

**Base Hit:** You went to all of your Sunday meetings.

**Home Run:** You were extra reverent so you could learn about Heavenly Father's plan.

**PRAY OFTEN**

**Foul Ball:** You liked to pray whenever someone reminded you to.

**Base Hit:** You made an effort to pray at least once a day.

**Home Run:** You prayed morning, noon, and night.

**DRESS MODESTLY**

**Foul Ball:** Your shorts were modest but not your swimming suit.

**Base Hit:** You wore your modest shirt even when it was hot.

**Home Run:** You went through your closet and got rid of all of your immodest clothing.

**BE HONEST**

**Foul Ball:** Without asking, you picked apricots off your neighbor's tree.

**Base Hit:** You thought about taking candy from the store but then decided not to steal.

**Home Run:** You always paid for things and returned what you borrowed.

**BE A FRIEND TO THE FRIENDLESS**

**Foul Ball:** You liked listening to your friends as they gossiped about others.

**Base Hit:** You said hi to those who didn't have friends.

**Home Run:** You invited the friendless to play with you and your friends.

**KEEP THE SABBATH HOLY**

**Foul Ball:** You shopped on Sunday because you forgot to get what you needed on Saturday.

**Base Hit:** You told your family you wanted to spend more time with them on Sunday.

**Home Run:** You made time for your family on Sunday and included them in your prayers.

**LOVE OTHERS**

**Foul Ball:** You told someone you wanted to play, but you never called.

**Base Hit:** You smiled at those who smiled at you.

**Home Run:** You were an ever-ready friend by being cheerful and listening.

**PAY TITHING**

**Foul Ball:** You liked to earn money and usually spent all of it.

**Base Hit:** You paid your tithing when your parents reminded you to.

**Home Run:** When you earned any money, you paid your tithing first.

**BELIEVE IN JESUS CHRIST**

**Foul Ball:** You wanted to believe in Jesus, but your friends talked you out of it.

**Base Hit:** You liked to hear the stories of Jesus when someone read them to you.

**Home Run:** You thought about Jesus each day and tried to do as He would do.

**HONOR YOUR PARENTS**

**Foul Ball:** You thought it was okay to do bad things as long as Mom and Dad didn't know.

**Base Hit:** You obeyed your mom by coming home right after school.

**Home Run:** You paid close attention to what your parents asked you to do, and you obeyed them.

**GET AN EDUCATION**

**Foul Ball:** You liked to stay home from school whenever you could.

**Base Hit:** After you played, you got your homework done most of the time.

**Home Run:** You spent most of your free time after school doing homework.

**HAVE FAMILY PRAYER**

**Foul Ball:** You said you were busy when it was time for family prayer.

**Base Hit:** You took your turn saying the family prayer.

**Home Run:** You gathered the family together each night for family prayer.

**KEEP A JOURNAL**

**Foul Ball:** You wrote in your journal once and then lost it.

**Base Hit:** You sometimes wrote your thoughts and feelings in your journal.

**Home Run:** You kept a weekly journal of your thoughts and feelings for your posterity to read.

OUT!

Take a ball off a base.

OUT!

Take a ball off a base.

OUT!

Take a ball off a base.

2ND BASE

3RD BASE

HOME RUN!
FOUL BALL
BASE HIT!
HOME RUN!
STRUCK OUT
BASE HIT!

## JUNE Theme: Follow Heavenly Father's Plan by Being Baptized and Confirmed

### *PRACTICE TIME:*

. **SCRIPTURE MEMORIZATION—3 Nephi 30:2** (shown left). Posters and cards are available to download from GospelGrabBag.com.
. **PRACTICE SONG—Sing "When I Am Baptized"** (*Children's Songbook*, 103) using the song visuals (shown right). These are available to download from GospelGrabBag.com.

### *SHARING TIME, Week 1: I will follow Jesus Christ by being baptized and confirmed and keeping my baptismal covenants.*

### *ACTIVITY: Follow in His Steps (Baptism and Covenants Walkabout)*

**OBJECTIVE:** Take children/youth on a walkabout to learn how we can follow in the footsteps of Jesus to "Be Baptized and Confirmed" and "Keep Baptismal Covenants." Each small step we take will help us follow Jesus in a big way (pointing to the large footprint).

**TO MAKE:** Copy, color, and cut out the images that follow. Use tape or magnets to mount visuals. Post the small feet word strips under the children's chairs or around the room. If copying feet in black and white, you will need to color the sandals with the star (*) symbol (found on the pattern page) a different color than the others.

**ACTIVITY:**

1. Talk to children/youth about the objective above and mount the large footprints on the board. Mount two different samples on the board (e.g.: (1) "Repent" is a small step we take to prepare us for baptism [place under **"Be Baptized and Confirmed"**]. (2) "Be Honest" is a small step we take to help us keep our baptismal covenant—living the gospel standards [place under **"Keep Baptismal Covenants"**]).
2. Have children/youth take turns finding a small foot word strip, reading it and placing it on the board under the right large footprint. Talk about the importance of each step.

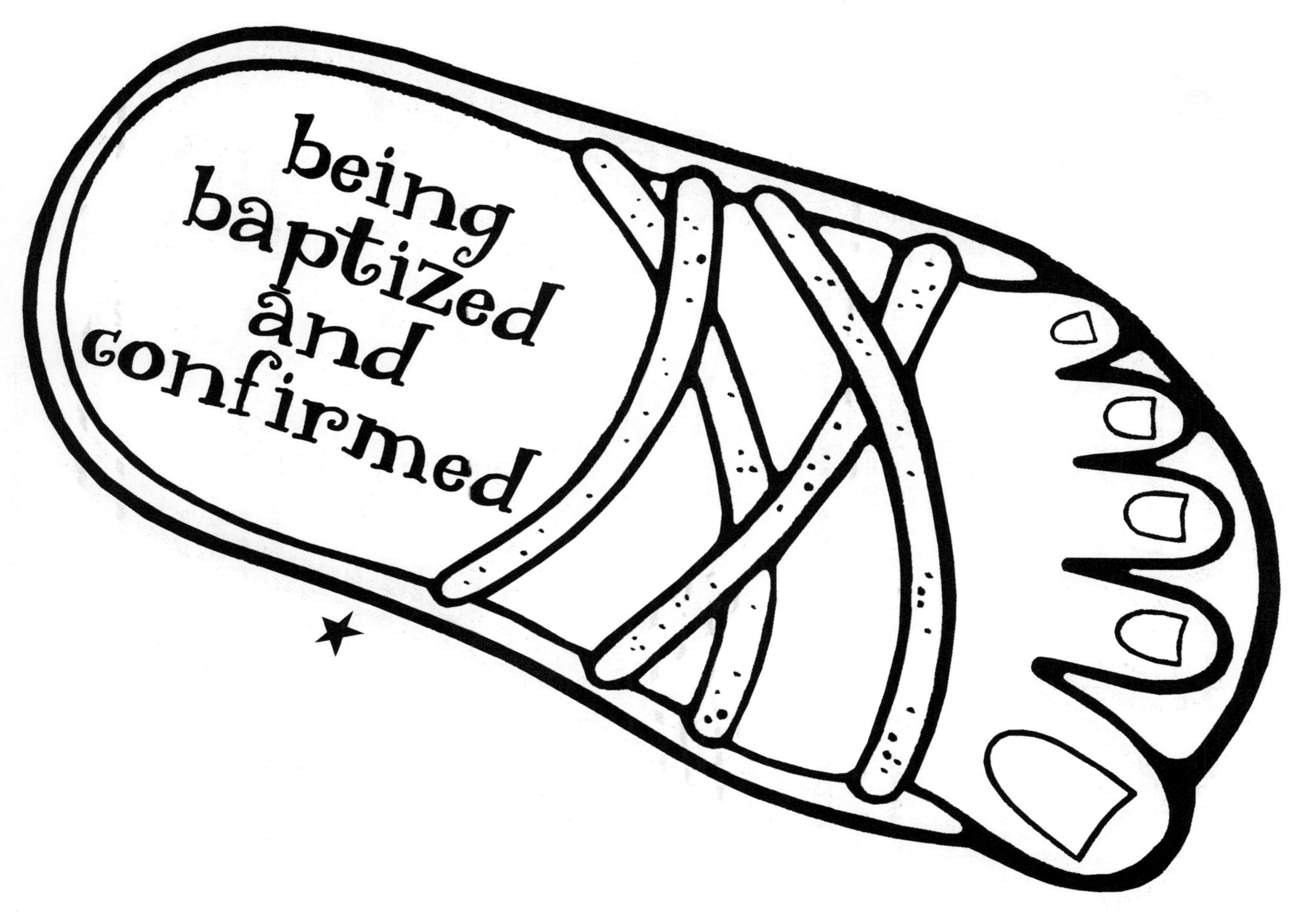
being
baptized
and
confirmed

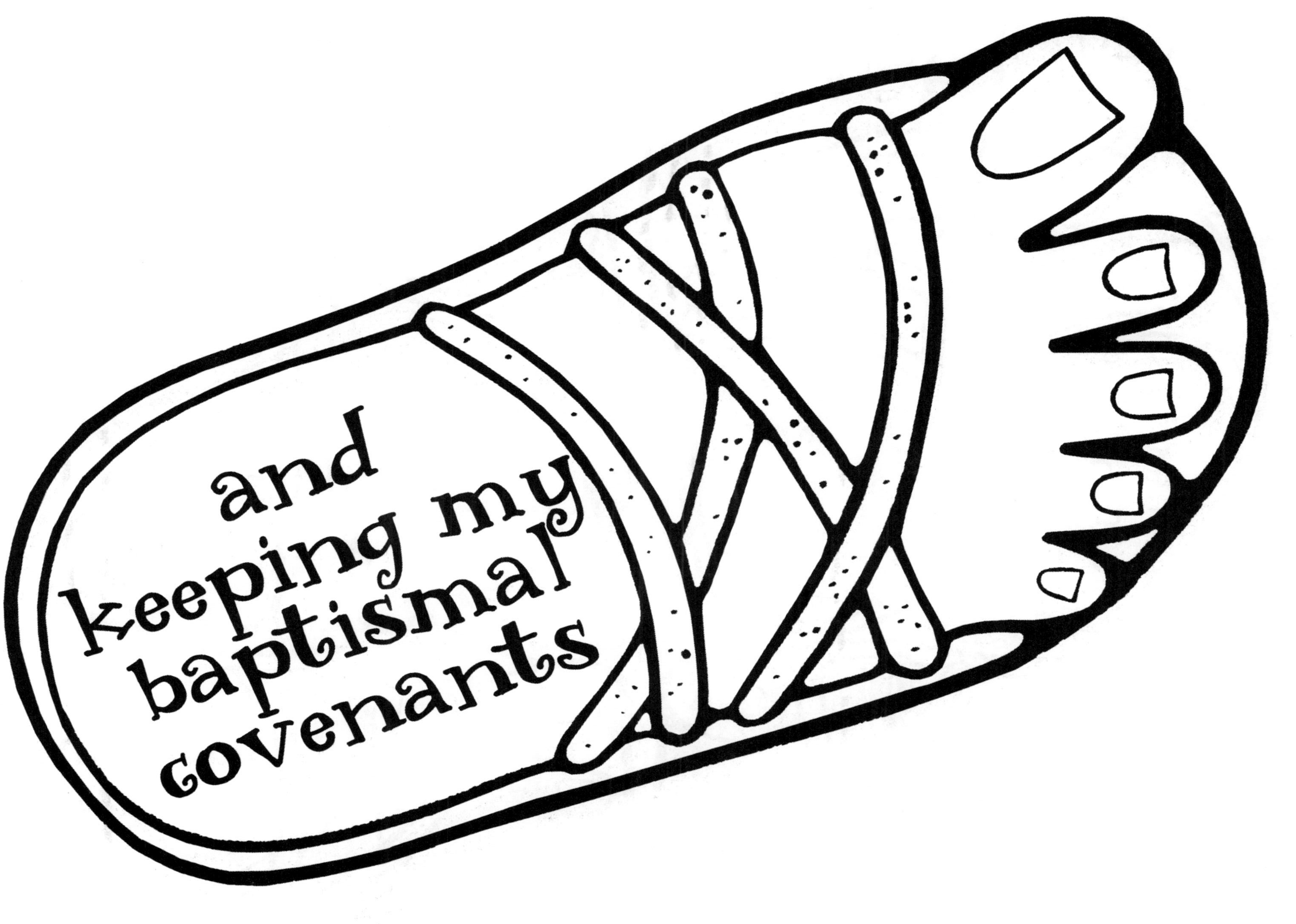
and
keeping my
baptismal
covenants

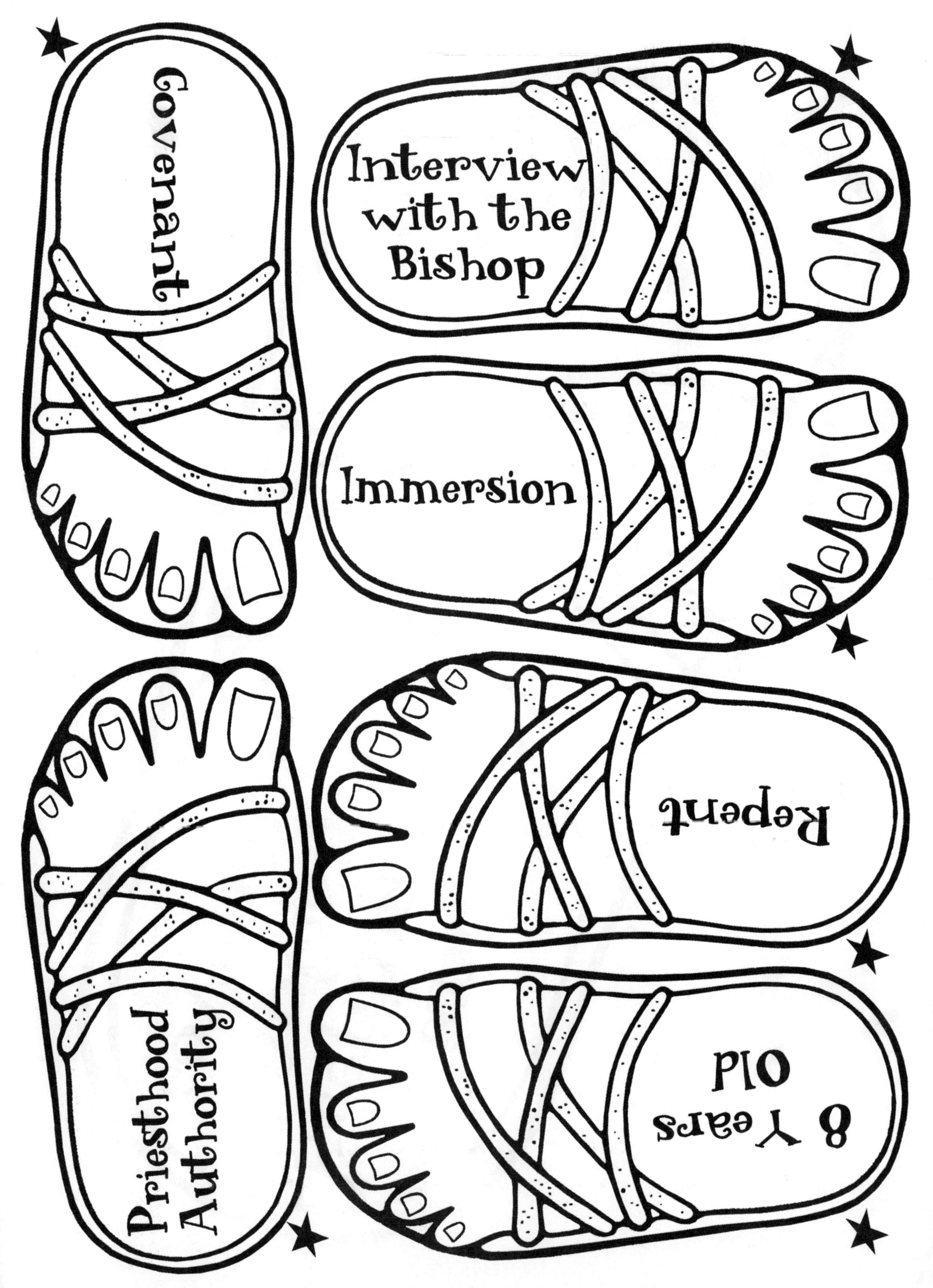
Covenant
Interview with the Bishop
Immersion
Repent
Priesthood Authority
8 Years Old

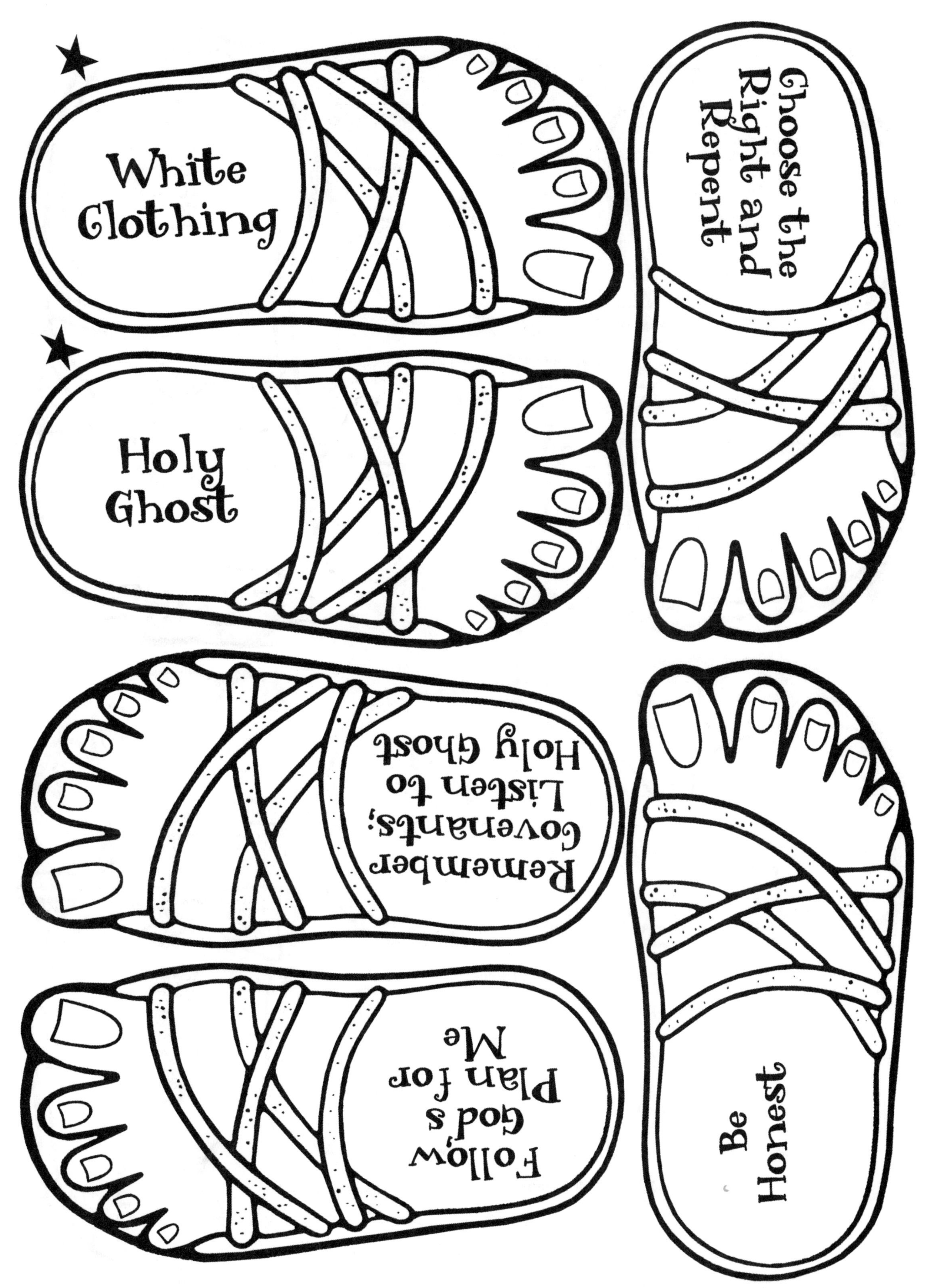
White Clothing
Holy Ghost
Choose the Right and Repent
Remember Covenants; Listen to Holy Ghost
Follow God's Plan for Me
Be Honest

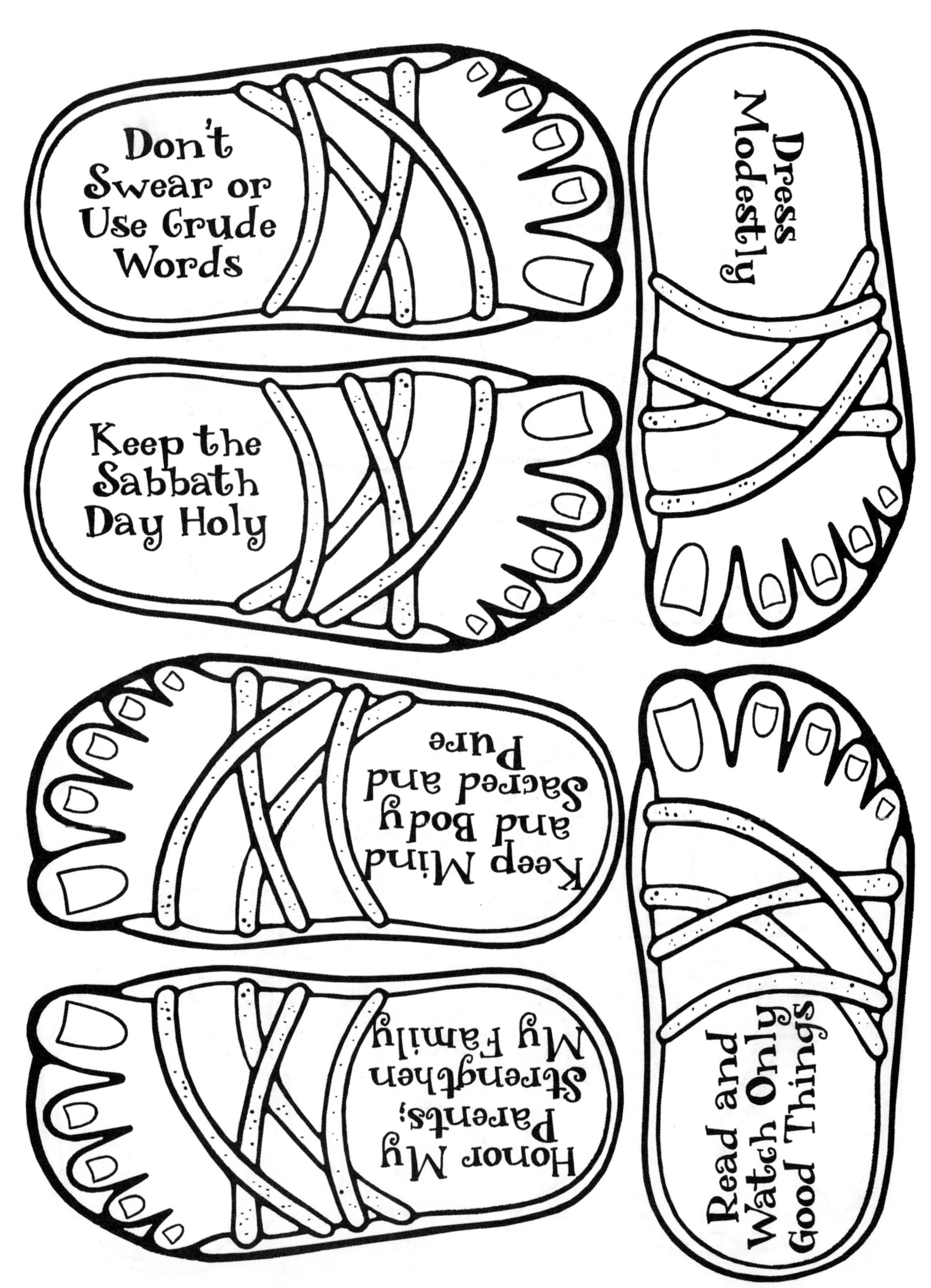
Don't Swear or Use Crude Words
Keep the Sabbath Day Holy
Dress Modestly
Keep Mind and Body Sacred and Pure
Honor My Parents; Strengthen My Family
Read and Watch Only Good Things

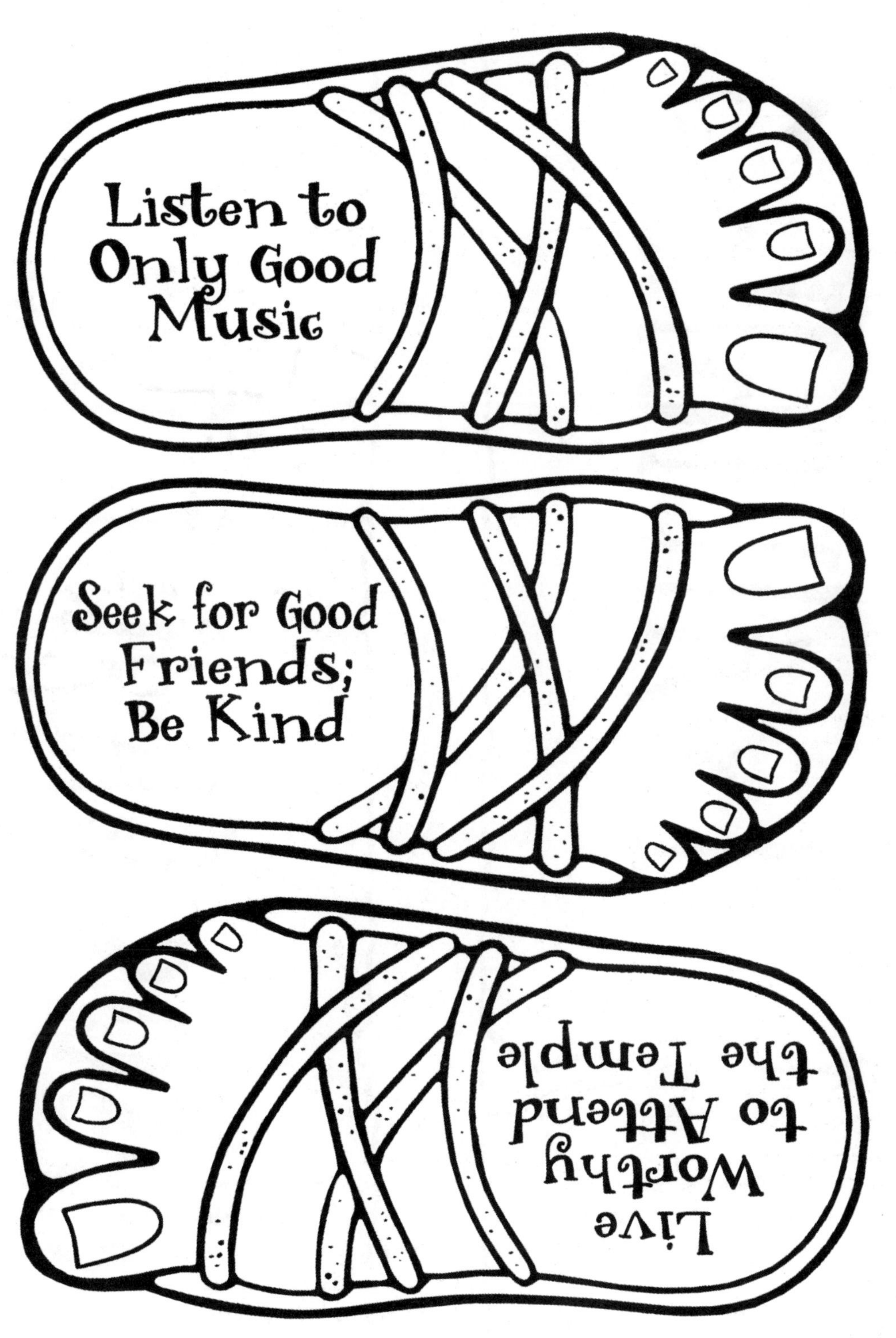
Listen to Only Good Music
Seek for Good Friends; Be Kind
Live Worthy to Attend the Temple

↓ Cut carefully along inside of dotted line.

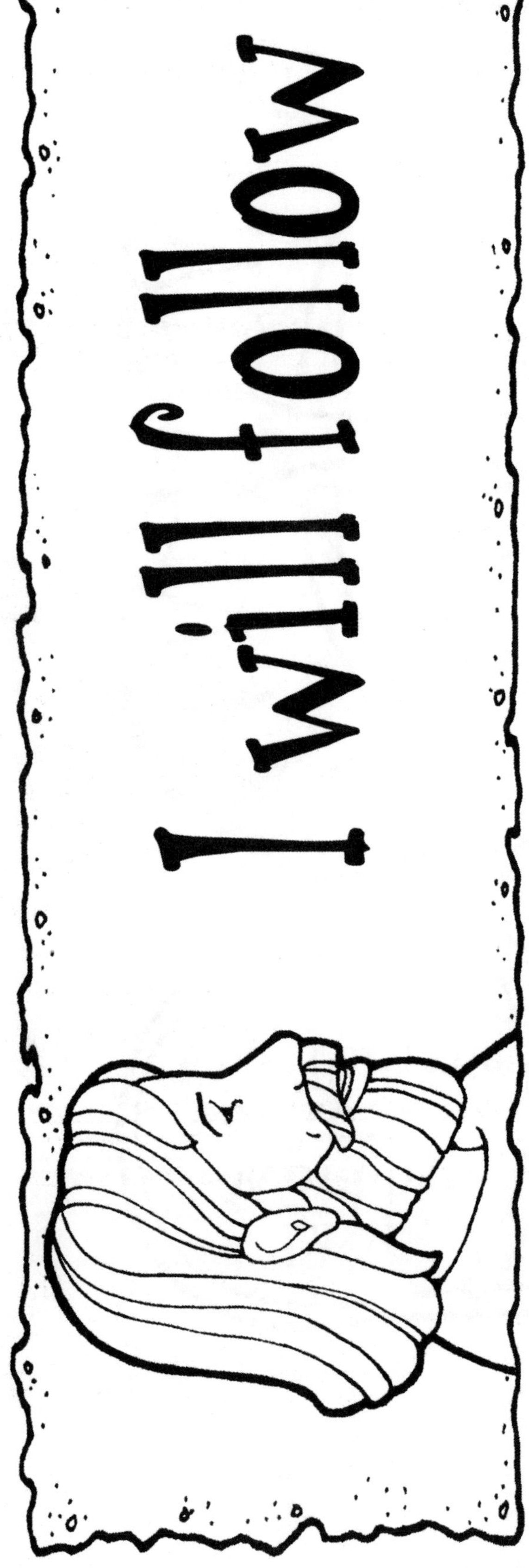


Jesus Christ by . . .

↕ Do not cut along dotted line.
Use this margin to mount other side.

## JUNE Theme: Follow Heavenly Father's Plan by Being Baptized and Confirmed

***PRACTICE TIME (download scripture & song visuals shown on p. 56 from GospelGrabBag.com)***

## *SHARING TIME, Week 2: If I live worthily, the Holy Ghost will help me choose the right.*

### *ACTIVITY: Trail to Holy Ghost Town GAME*

**OBJECTIVE:** Help children know that through choosing the right, the Holy Ghost will be a part of their life to prompt, teach, and guide them.

**TO MAKE:** Copy, color, and cut out the images that follow. Laminate. You will need a die to toss and double-stick tape or magnets (to mount visuals on the board).

**TO SET UP GAME:** Tape the **Death Valley** sign on the bottom and **Holy Ghost Town** at the top of the board. Tape the rock signs, making a trail to and from the two signs. Tape the Start sign on the trail as shown.

**TO PLAY:** Tell children, "We are going to play a game called **Trail to Holy Ghost Town**. Let's imagine we are going to a special town filled with good people who choose the right. They listen to the promptings of the Holy Ghost, which makes this town a happy town. Let's imagine that those who do wrong actions and do not repent of these actions go to **Death Valley**, a place where the Holy Ghost cannot dwell. The first team to get to Holy Ghost Town wins the game!"

1. Divide children into two teams and give each team a Boot marker to place on the Dynamite/Start position on the board. Use double-stick tape to keep markers on the board.
2. Flip a coin to determine which team goes first.
3. Teams take turns rolling a die and moving that number of rocks along the trail, following "move forward" or "move backward" signs on rocks.
4. When players land on **Trail Mix** rock, draw a situation from the **Trail Mix** container, read the situation, and move forward and backward as indicated on the card. Tape the card to the board or use magnets to mount.
5. If you land on **Death Valley**, roll the die on your next turn to get back on the trail.
6. Winners get there first!

64–73 (Instructions & Visuals)

You say your prayers morning and night to keep heaven in sight (move ahead 1).
You pray and ask Heavenly Father to help you stay on the strait and narrow path (move ahead 1).
It's time to get ready for church, but you tell your parents you are sick when you are just tired (move back 2).
Your parents ask you to feed your baby brother, but you feed yourself first (move back 1).
You tell your teacher you read your assignment when you forgot (move back 1).
You read the scriptures each day and learn about the gospel of Jesus Christ (move ahead 2).
You take turns on the playground and give the other children a chance to play (move ahead 1).
You want a bike like your friend's so you beg your mom to buy one when you have no money (move back 1).

You say excuse me, thank you, and please (move ahead 1).
It is not Thanksgiving, but you thank Heavenly Father anyway (move ahead 1).
You are in a hurry to get to school, and you don't stop to help a boy who fell off his bike (move back 1).
Your mother asks you to take a get-well card to a neighbor on your way to play, but you forget (move back 1).
You are asked to rake the leaves and help with the garden, but you ride your bike instead (move back 1).
You kick the dog when she gets in your way (move back 2).
You tell your sister she did a good job (move ahead 1).
Your mother asks you to wear your coat, but you leave it home on purpose (move back 1).

You like to jump on the trampoline and share it with your friends (move ahead 1).
You felt like yelling at your brother when he yelled at you, but you didn't (move ahead 2).
You like to throw rocks at cats, dogs, and birds (move back 2).
It's your turn at the drinking fountain, but you let a smaller child in front of you (move ahead 1).
Your friends want you to take some candy at the store without paying, but you say, "no" (move ahead 1).
You are at a friend's party and decide to take one of his birthday presents home (move back 2).
You work hard to get your homework done so you don't have to do school work on Sunday (move ahead 1).
You are tempted to smoke a cigarette, but you don't (move ahead 2).

You take tithing money and spend it on a new bike (move back 1).
You are leaving with your family for a few days, and you forget to put extra food out for the dog (move back 2).
You raise your hand to answer questions in Primary class (move ahead 1).
You play with a non-member friend but don't invite him to the Primary activity (move back 1).
You are nice to your sister when mom is around, but when she's gone, you are unkind (move back 1).
You read a Book of Mormon story to a friend (move ahead 1).
You want to give a talk in Primary but never raise your hand (move back 1).
You are asked to help lead the younger children in a game, and you say "yes" (move ahead 1).

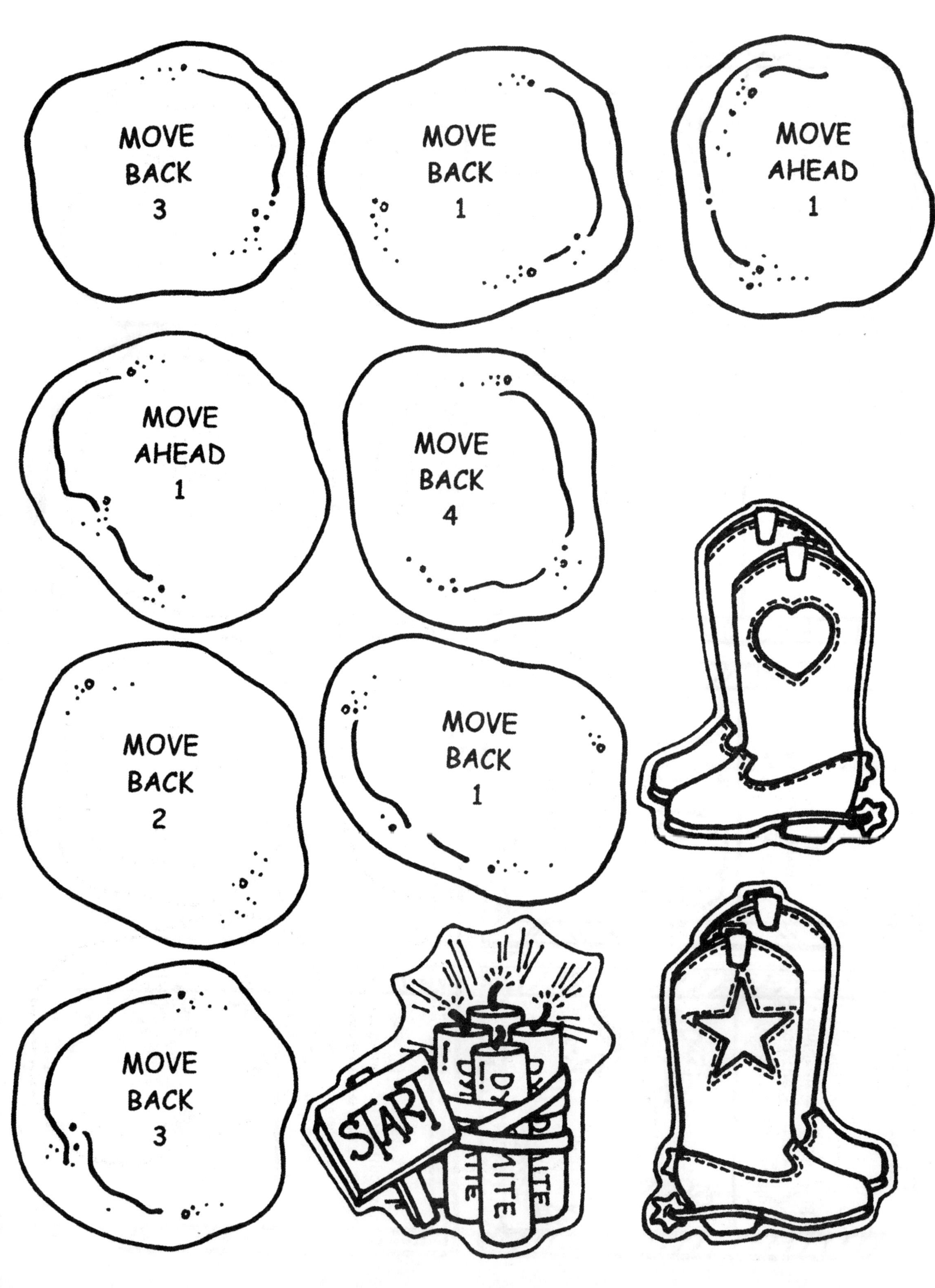
MOVE
BACK
3
MOVE
BACK
1
MOVE
AHEAD
1
MOVE
AHEAD
1
MOVE
BACK
4
MOVE
BACK
2
MOVE
BACK
1
MOVE
BACK
3
START

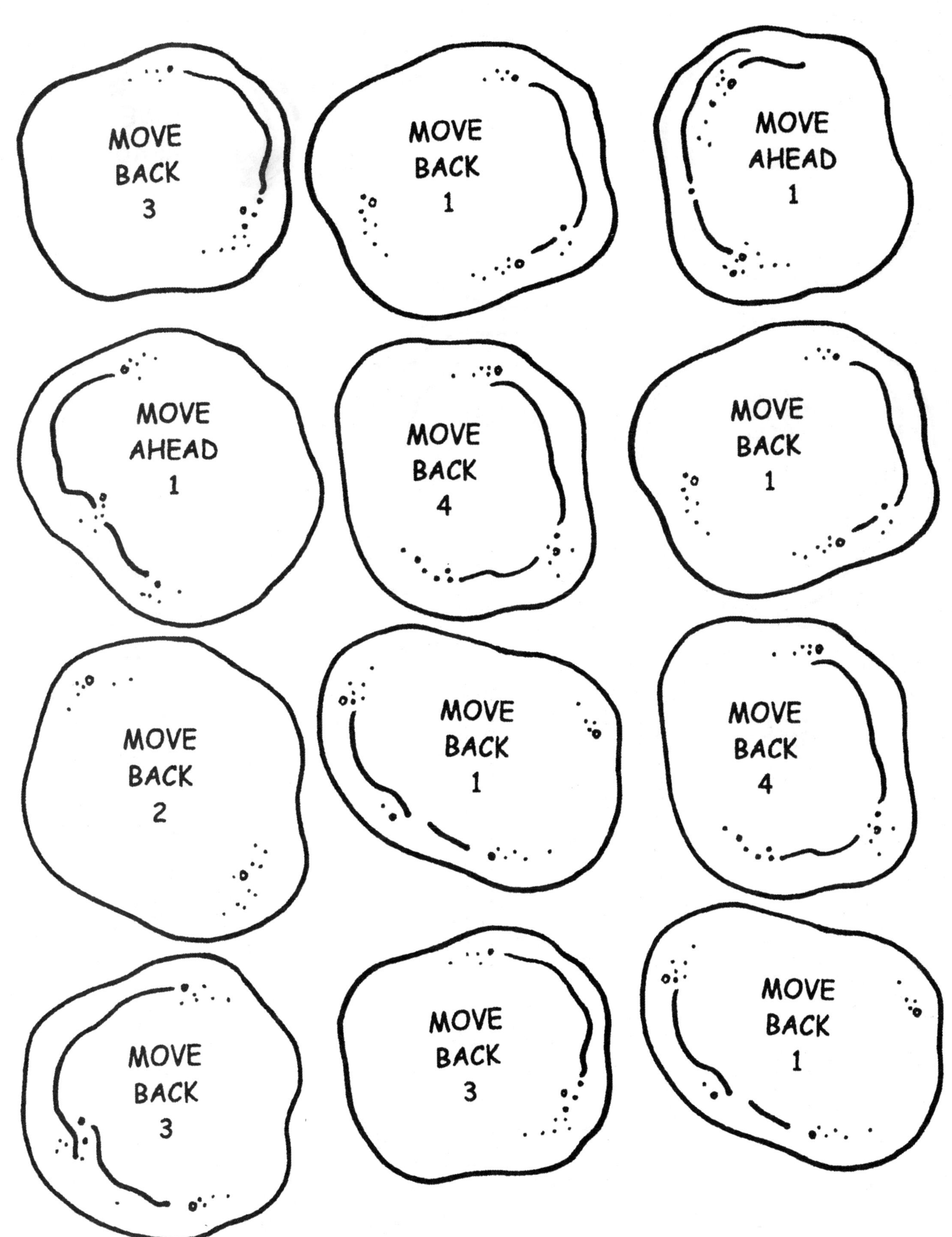
MOVE
BACK
3
MOVE
BACK
1
MOVE
AHEAD
1
MOVE
AHEAD
1
MOVE
BACK
4
MOVE
BACK
1
MOVE
BACK
2
MOVE
BACK
1
MOVE
BACK
4
MOVE
BACK
3
MOVE
BACK
3
MOVE
BACK
1

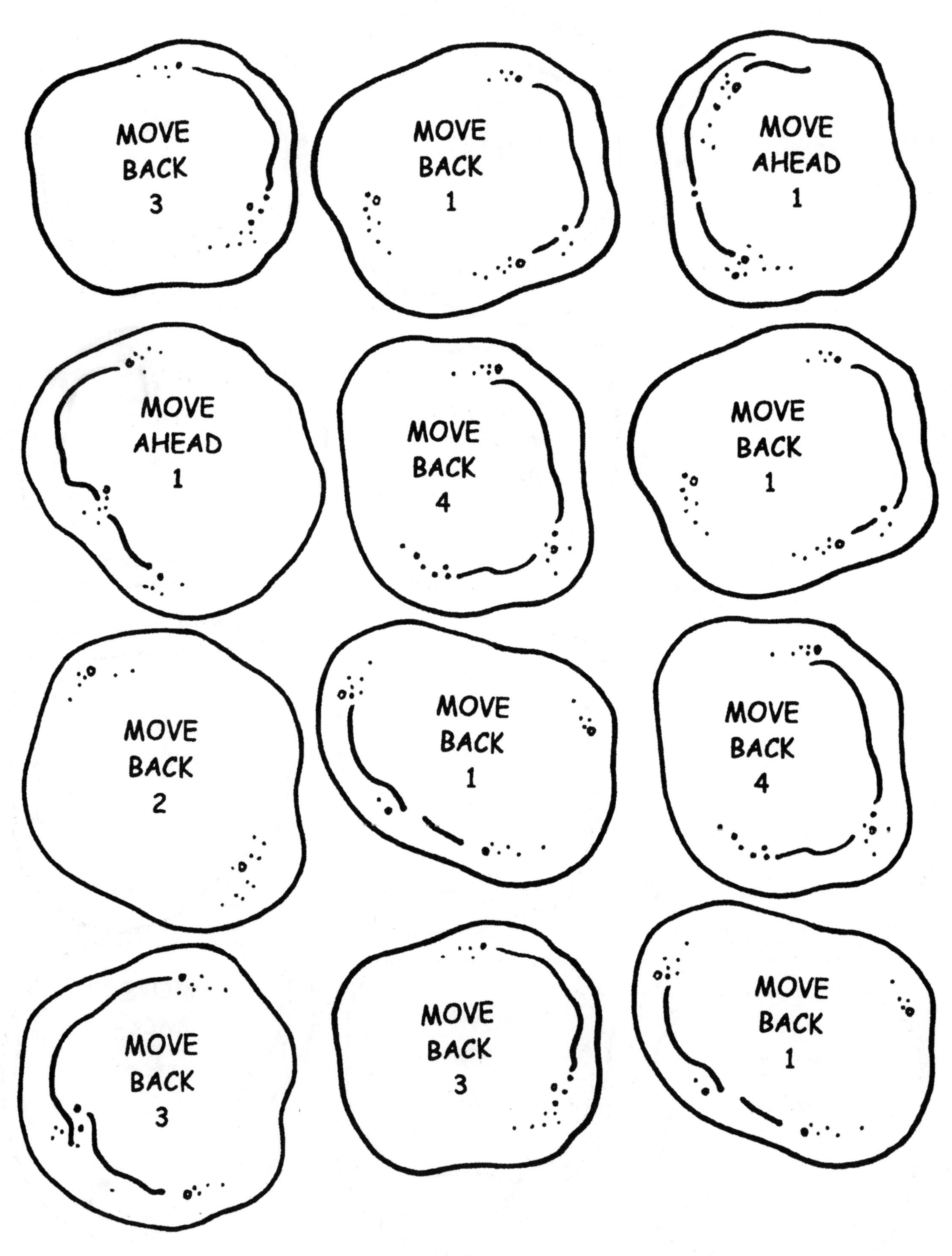
MOVE
BACK
3
MOVE
BACK
1
MOVE
AHEAD
1
MOVE
AHEAD
1
MOVE
BACK
4
MOVE
BACK
1
MOVE
BACK
2
MOVE
BACK
1
MOVE
BACK
4
MOVE
BACK
3
MOVE
BACK
3
MOVE
BACK
1

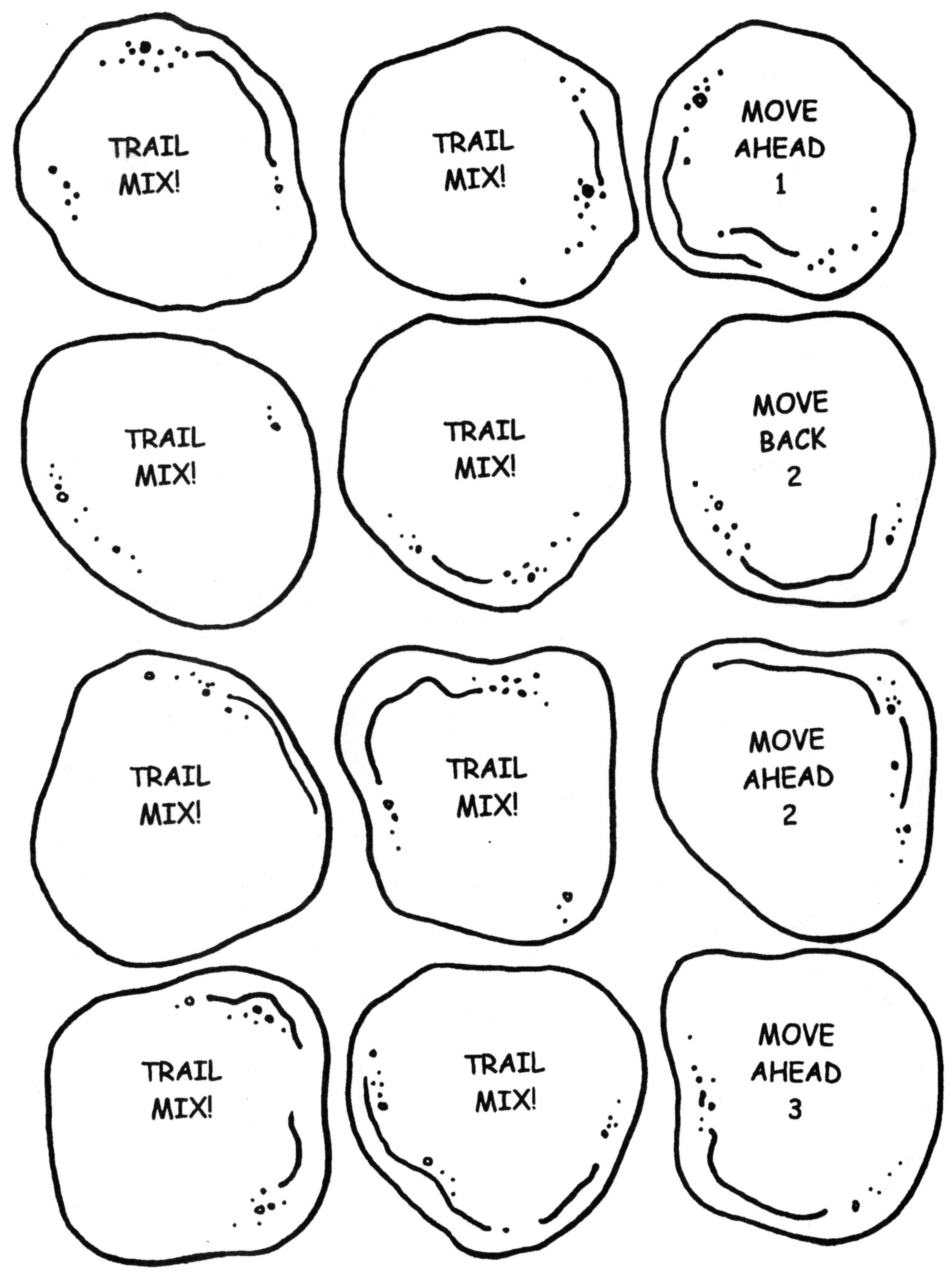
TRAIL MIX!
TRAIL MIX!
MOVE AHEAD 1
TRAIL MIX!
TRAIL MIX!
MOVE BACK 2
TRAIL MIX!
TRAIL MIX!
MOVE AHEAD 2
TRAIL MIX!
TRAIL MIX!
MOVE AHEAD 3

# DEATH VALLEY

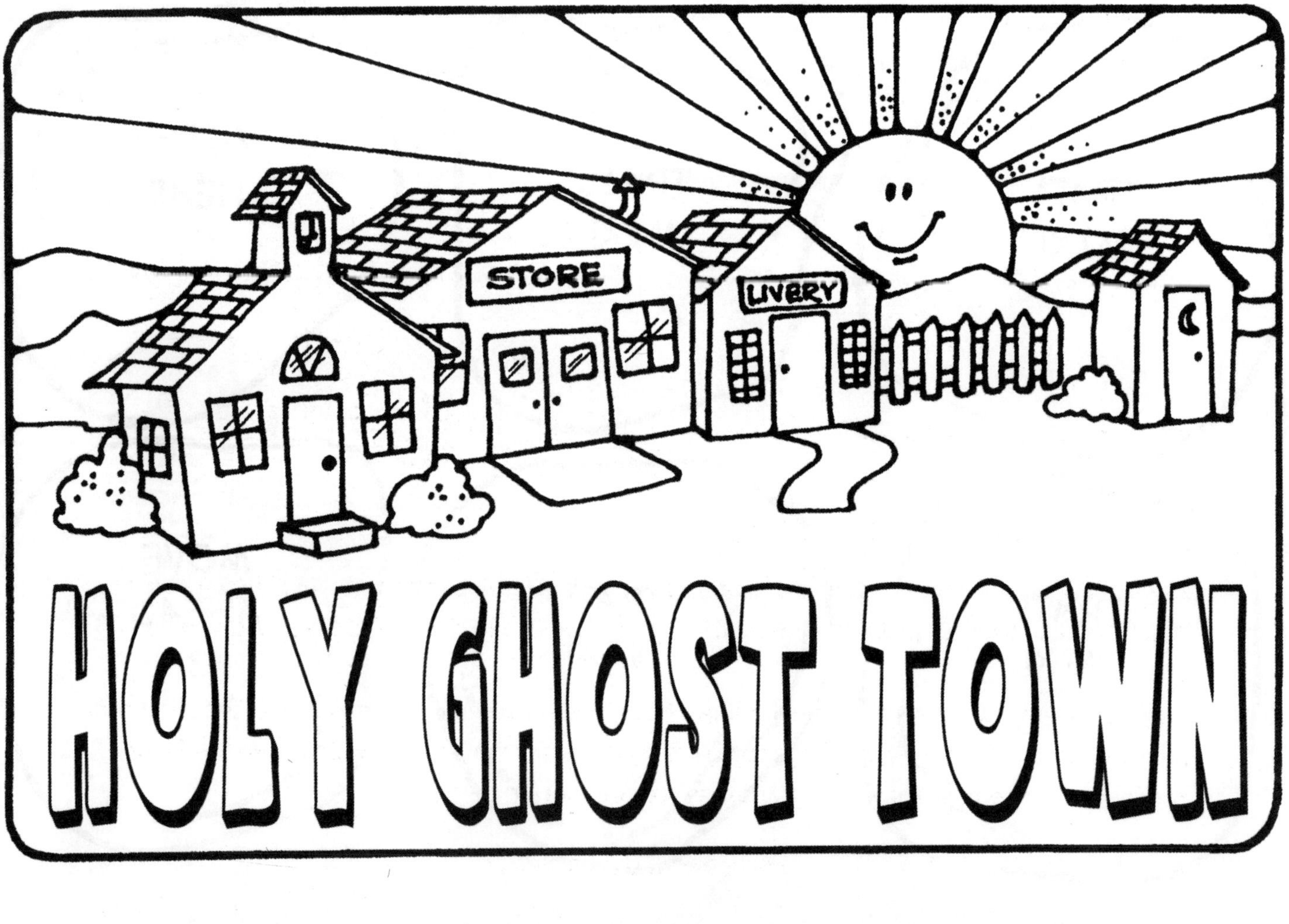

STORE

LIVERY

# HOLY GHOST TOWN

## JULY Theme: Families Are Part of Heavenly Father's Plan

### *PRACTICE TIME:*

**. SCRIPTURE MEMORIZATION—"The family is ordained of God" ("The Family: A Proclamation to the World," paragraph 7)** (shown left). Posters and cards are available to download from GospelGrabBag.com.

**. PRACTICE SONG—Sing "Families Can Be Together Forever"** (*Children's Songbook*, 188) using the song visuals (shown right). These are available to download from GospelGrabBag.com.

### *SHARING TIME, Week 2: Family prayer, family scripture study, and family home evening can strengthen my family.*

### *ACTIVITY: We Can Build a Happy Home (Tools to Build Quiz)*

**OBJECTIVE:** Help children/youth learn how they can build a happy home with three important tools: family prayer, family scripture study, and family home evening.

**TO MAKE:** Copy, color, and cut out the images that follow. Use tape or magnets to mount visuals. Mount pictures on the board as shown with hearts under the children's chairs or around the room.

**ACTIVITY:**

1. Place the tools under the home and talk about each tool that helps us build a happy home. When we face trials or problems come up, we can choose one or more of these tools to help us.
2. Ask children/youth to take turns finding a heart and reading the situation. Then tell what tool they would use to help. Point to the tool and say it: Family Prayer, Family Scripture Study, or Family Home Evening. Some situations may require more than one tool.

Cut carefully along inside of dotted line.

e Can
uild a
appy
ome!

Do not cut along dotted line. Use this margin to mount other side.

Family
Scripture Study
Family Home Evening
Family Prayer

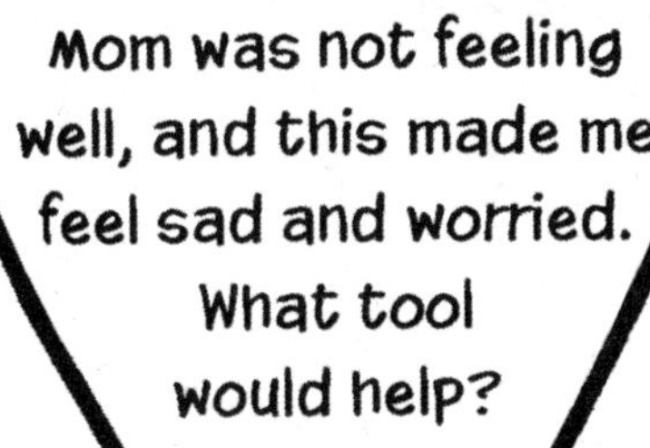

Mom was not feeling well, and this made me feel sad and worried. What tool would help?

Every day, my family drives on the busy roads, and I want them to be safe. What tool would help?

I want to have the Holy Ghost to guide me each day to make right choices. What tool would help?

I want the missionaries preaching the gospel to do well. What tool would help?

I am going to take a test at school tomorrow, and I need Heavenly Father to help me. What tool would help?

My family wants the prophet to have health and safety. What tool would help?

My family needs to grow closer together. What tool would help?

My friends sometimes ask me to do something that I feel is not right. What tool would help?

Most of my family is good at sports, but my brother wants to learn to hit the ball to show his friends. What tool would help?

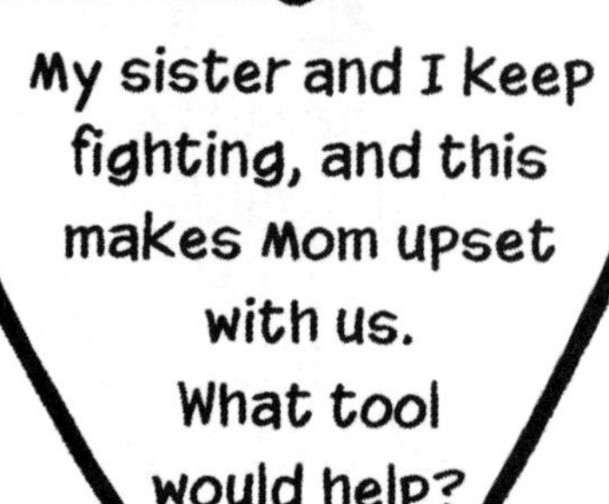

My sister and I keep fighting, and this makes Mom upset with us.
What tool would help?

I would like to learn to make special treats to share with my family and friends.
What tool would help?

My friend has asked me what I believe, but I don't know what to tell her.
What tool would help?

In Primary, we are asked to learn and recite the Articles of Faith.
What tool would help?

I love to learn the stories of Jesus.
What tool would help?

I want to gain a testimony so I can bear it in fast and testimony meeting.
What tool would help?

I need to feel close to the Spirit.
What tool would help?

I would like to learn to live the Ten Commandments.
What tool would help?

I must prepare a talk to give in Primary next week but don't know what to say.
What tool would help?

## AUGUST Theme: Heavenly Father Hears and Answers My Prayers

### *PRACTICE TIME:*

. **SCRIPTURE MEMORIZATION—D&C 112:10** (shown left). Posters and cards are available to download from GospelGrabBag.com.
. **PRACTICE SONG—Sing "A Child's Prayer"** (*Children's Songbook*, 12–13) using the song visuals (shown right). These are available to download from GospelGrabBag.com.

### *SHARING TIME, Week 2: Heavenly Father wants me to pray to Him often—anytime, anywhere.*

### *ACTIVITY: Turn to Answered Prayers (Scripture Stories Wheel)*

**OBJECTIVE:** Help children learn **who** in the scriptures prayed, **what** they prayed about, and **how** prayers were answered, matching up images to show and tell.

**TO MAKE:** Copy, color, and cut out the images that follow. Laminate puzzle pieces.

**Matching Visuals Summary:** See unmatched visuals (shown): Alma (people sleeping, person tied up), Enos (praying by stars, arms stretched out), Shadrach . . . (two fire scenes), Joseph Smith (churches, Heavenly Father and Jesus), Nephi (ship, promised land) King Mosiah (praying, preaching).

80–89 (Instructions & Visuals)

Page 2 (Turn to Answered Prayers—Scripture Stories Wheel)

**TO MOUNT CIRCLES ON POSTER:**

1. You will need two pieces of poster paper—one to make the center circle and the 13" middle circle, and one to make the 19" outer circle.
2. To draw a circle, use a pin or tack, a string, and a pencil or marker. Tie the string around the pencil or marker, find a center point, and push the pin or thumbtack through the poster paper. Measure out half the distance (13"—draw 7.5" from the center, and 19"—draw 9.5" from the center). Tie the string for the appropriate measurement around the pin or tack, then draw the circle.
3. Mount illustration for the center, then cut out all three circles. Connect the three circles in the center with a paper fastener, using the pinholes. With the center circle as a guide, draw lines from the center circle through the second and third circles, as shown.
4. Cut out the illustrations for the 13" and 19" circles. Using the visual (preview on the previous page) as a guide, glue- or spray-mount the illustrations in the order they appear. Make sure you do not line up all the stories, since once a story has been "dialed," you don't want all the other stories to line up as well. This will ensure that they are already mixed up before the next clue is read.

**ACTIVITY:**

1. Tell children, "Because Heavenly Father loves us, He allows us to talk with Him. **He is as close as a prayer, and we can pray to Him anytime and anywhere.** When we pray, we should first thank Him for our blessings, then ask Him for the help we need. But we must choose the right so we can be worthy of His blessings (2 Nephi 32:9). In the scriptures, we learn of honorable people who prayed and how their prayers were answered."

2. Point to the circles and show children the story cards that tell **WHO** in the scriptures prayed (inside circle), **WHAT** they prayed about (center circle), and **HOW** their prayers were answered (outside circle).

*Option 1:* Divide the stories among the classes. Then children can read the story together as a class and come up to tell the story, turning the circle so the puzzle pieces match for that story.

*Option 2:* The leader calls a child up and gives him or her a KEY WORD (found in a box—make these up ahead of time). If the child knows the story, he or she can quickly turn the circles to match up the parts of the story (WHO, WHAT, and HOW) with one clue. If not, the leader can give a second clue, then a third clue if necessary. If the child still cannot make the match, he or she forfeits to another child (or the other team), who gets a chance to earn the points missed.

Enos
Alma
Nephi
Joseph Smith
King Mosiah
Shadrach, Meshach, and Abed-nego

CHURCH

ZZZZ..

| WHO in the scriptures? | HOW were their prayers answered? |
|---|---|
| Alma and his people had an **ENEMY**, Amulon. The Lamanite king made Amulon the ruler over Alma's people. Amulon knew that Alma believed the words spoken by the prophet Abinadi while in King Noah's court, so Amulon caused that his children should persecute Alma's children, making them work as their **SLAVES**. | God heard their prayers and strengthened them, making their burdens seem light and helping the people be cheerful and patient. The Lord said, "On the morrow I will deliver you out of bondage." Alma's people gathered their flocks and grain during the night. In the morning,"the Lord caused a **DEEP SLEEP** to come upon the Lamanites," and Alma was able to lead his people into the wilderness to safety. They "poured out their thanks to God because he had been merciful unto them, and eased their burdens, and had delivered them out of bondage." Twelve days later, Alma and his people arrived in the land of Zarahemla, "and king Mosiah did also receive them with joy." (See Mosiah 23:39; 24:8-25.) |
| WHAT did they pray about? | WHO in the scriptures? |
| Their afflictions were so great that "they began to cry mightily to God." Amulon commanded them to stop their cries, putting guards around to put to death any who prayed. They did not pray aloud but **PRAYED IN THEIR HEARTS**, and the Lord heard them in their afflictions. God said, "Lift up your heads and be of good comfort, for I know of the covenant which ye have made unto me; and I will covenant with my people and deliver them out of bondage." He said he would ease their burdens, "that ye may stand as witnesses for me hereafter." The Lord knew they would stand for the right. | Enos was the grandson of Lehi, who was the son of Jacob, Nephi's brother (see Jacob 1:1–2, 8; 7:27). Enos kept the plates and wrote on them after his father died. One day while **HUNTING** in the forest, Enos thought about his father's teachings and wanted to be forgiven of his sins (see Enos 1:3–4). He knelt and prayed all day and was still praying when night came. |
| | WHAT did he pray about? |
| | Enos asked Heavenly Father to **FORGIVE HIM** of his sins. He said his soul hungered for peace. |

| | |
|---|---|
| HOW were his prayers answered?<br>Enos heard a voice saying: "Enos, thy sins are forgiven thee, and thou shalt be blessed" (Enos 1:5). Enos knew that God could not lie, and his "**GUILT** was swept away" (Enos 1:6). God told him, "Because of thy faith in Christ, whom thou hast never before heard nor seen . . . thy faith hath made thee whole" (Enos 1:8). The Lord told him, " I will grant unto thee according to thy desires, because of thy faith" (Enos 1:12).<br>(See Enos 1:1–17.) | HOW were their prayers answered?<br>The king looked into the furnace and saw four men walking around in the fire. One of the men was an angel of God that saved Shadrach, Meshach, and Abed-nego from the flames. The king shouted their names and told them to come out of the furnace. The fire had not hurt them or burned their hair or clothes. They didn't even smell like **SMOKE**. The king made a new law that no one could say bad things about the God of Israel—that only the true God could have saved the men from the fire. The king honored these men. (See Daniel 3.) |
| WHO in the scriptures?<br>In the Bible we read about Shadrach, Meshach, and Abed-nego, who would not pray to the **IDOL** made of gold. They prayed to the true God instead. The king of Babylon had made the idol and told the people to pray to the idol or they would be burned in a fiery furnace. | WHO in the scriptures?<br>When Joseph Smith was 14 years old, many churches claimed to be the true Church of Jesus Christ. Joseph read in the Bible: "If any of you **LACK WISDOM**, let him ask of God" (James 1:5). |
| WHAT did they pray about?<br>The king was angry when someone told him that Shadrach, Meshach, and Abed-nego were praying to God and not to the idol. He told them they would be burned in the **FURNACE**, but they were not afraid, because they knew God would save them. The king's servants built a very hot fire in the furnace. It was so hot that the servants died when they threw Shadrach, Meshach, and Abed-nego inside. | WHAT did he pray about?<br>He needed to know **WHICH CHURCH** he should join, so he decided to ask God. He went into the woods near his home to pray. As he knelt in prayer, Satan tried to stop him from praying. So he prayed harder, asking Heavenly Father to help him. |

HOW were his prayers answered?
Heavenly Father and Jesus Christ appeared to Joseph Smith in a pillar of light. Heavenly Father pointed to Jesus, saying, "This is My Beloved Son, Hear Him!" Joseph asked Them which church to join. Jesus told him not to join any of them, as they were all wrong. Three years later, the angel Moroni visited Joseph, telling him where **GOLD PLATES** were hidden that contained a sacred record. Joseph went to the Hill Cumorah and looked at the plates. Four years later, he received the plates and translated them into the Book of Mormon. This book tells about the people who lived in America many years ago and about Jesus Christ. Joseph restored Jesus Christ's true Church on the earth. (See Joseph Smith—History 1:1–71.)

WHO in the scriptures?
Nephi followed his father, the prophet Lehi, when he asked him to **LEAVE HIS HOME** in Jerusalem and go into the wilderness. Then he did as he was asked and went back to Jerusalem to obtain the sacred records. Then the family camped by the sea.

WHAT did he pray about?
Nephi went to the mountain many times to pray for help, to know how he could take his family to the **PROMISED LAND**.

HOW were his prayers answered?
Nephi was told to **BUILD A SHIP** to carry his family across the sea to the promised land. He was told where to find the metal and tools needed to build the ship. Nephi's older brothers Laman and Lemuel tried to stop him from building the ship, and they tried to hurt him. The Lord told Nephi to touch them and when he did the Lord shocked them. They repented and helped Nephi and their brother Sam build the ship, a strong ship that would withstand the winds and take them to the promised land. (See 1 Nephi 17:7–55; 18:1–8.)

WHO in the scriptures?
In the Book of Mormon, we read about a Nephite king named Mosiah, who was the son of the righteous King Benjamin. Ammon and King Mosiah's other sons wanted to go on a mission to preach to the Lamanites, who often wanted to kill the Nephites. The king was worried for their **SAFETY**.

WHAT did he pray about?
"And king Mosiah went and inquired of the Lord if he should **LET HIS SONS GO** up among the Lamanites to preach the word" (Mosiah 28:6).

HOW were his prayers answered?
"And the Lord said unto Mosiah: Let them go up, for many shall believe on their words, and they shall have eternal life; and I will deliver thy sons out of the hands of the Lamanites. And it came to pass that Mosiah granted that they might go and do according to their request. And they took their journey into the wilderness to go up to **PREACH** the word among the Lamanites" (Mosiah 28:7–9).

## SEPTEMBER Theme: I Will Serve God with All My Heart, Might, Mind, and Strength

### *PRACTICE TIME:*

. **SCRIPTURE MEMORIZATION—D&C 59:5** (shown left). Posters and cards are available to download from GospelGrabBag.com.

. **PRACTICE SONG—Sing "I'm Trying to Be Like Jesus"** (*Children's Songbook*, 78) using the song visuals (shown right). These are available to download from GospelGrabBag.com.

### *SHARING TIME, Week 1:* *Jesus taught us how to serve others.*

### *ACTIVITY: I Will Follow Jesus (Service Road Game)*

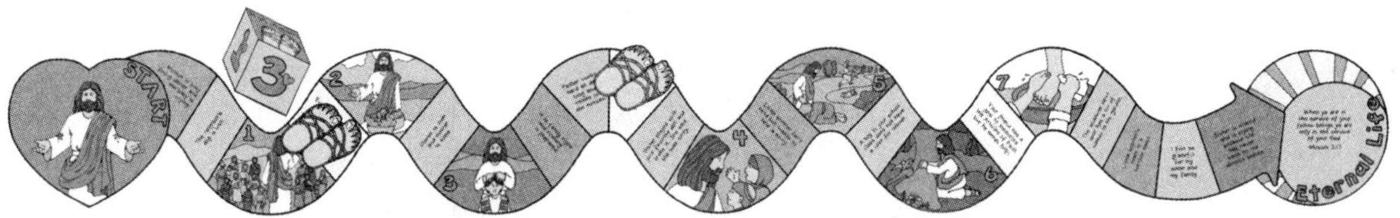


**OBJECTIVE:** Help children learn to be like Jesus by learning how He served others and how they can be of service.

**TO MAKE:** Copy, color, and cut out the images and stories that follow. Use tape or magnets to mount visuals. Glue service road parts together. To create block, fold die and tabs and glue where indicated. When coloring feet markers, color sandals different colors (to specify teams).

**ACTIVITY:**

1. Ahead of time, assign different Jesus Service Stories 1–7 to classes to read aloud when their number is called.
2. Post the service road and tell children/youth, "Our faith in Jesus Christ grows as we learn how He served others and as we look for ways we can serve. When we serve others, we are serving Jesus (review Mosiah 2:17). DOWNLOAD below.

Tell youth: "If we live a life of service, we can become like Jesus. Then we—like Jesus—can have eternal life and live with Heavenly Father again someday."

**TO PLAY THE GAME:**

1. Divide children/youth into two teams and have them take turns rolling the die block and moving the team's feet marker forward from the START position, according to the number on the die.
2. If a player moves to the "Jesus Story" position on the board, read the number aloud. Have the one who has that story number present the story and tell how we can serve like Jesus. *Note:* If the second team that follows lands on the same story, have them paraphrase the story that was told or have the class read the story again. If they can tell the story because they listened well, give them a chance to play again.
3. If a player moves to a situation position on the board, have them read the situation and tell how they can serve.
4. Move to ETERNAL LIFE, and repeat the game until time is up. If a team lands on a "Jesus Story" or situation they have landed on before, have them move to the next one.
5. The first team to get to ETERNAL LIFE wins.

90–99 (Instructions & Visuals)

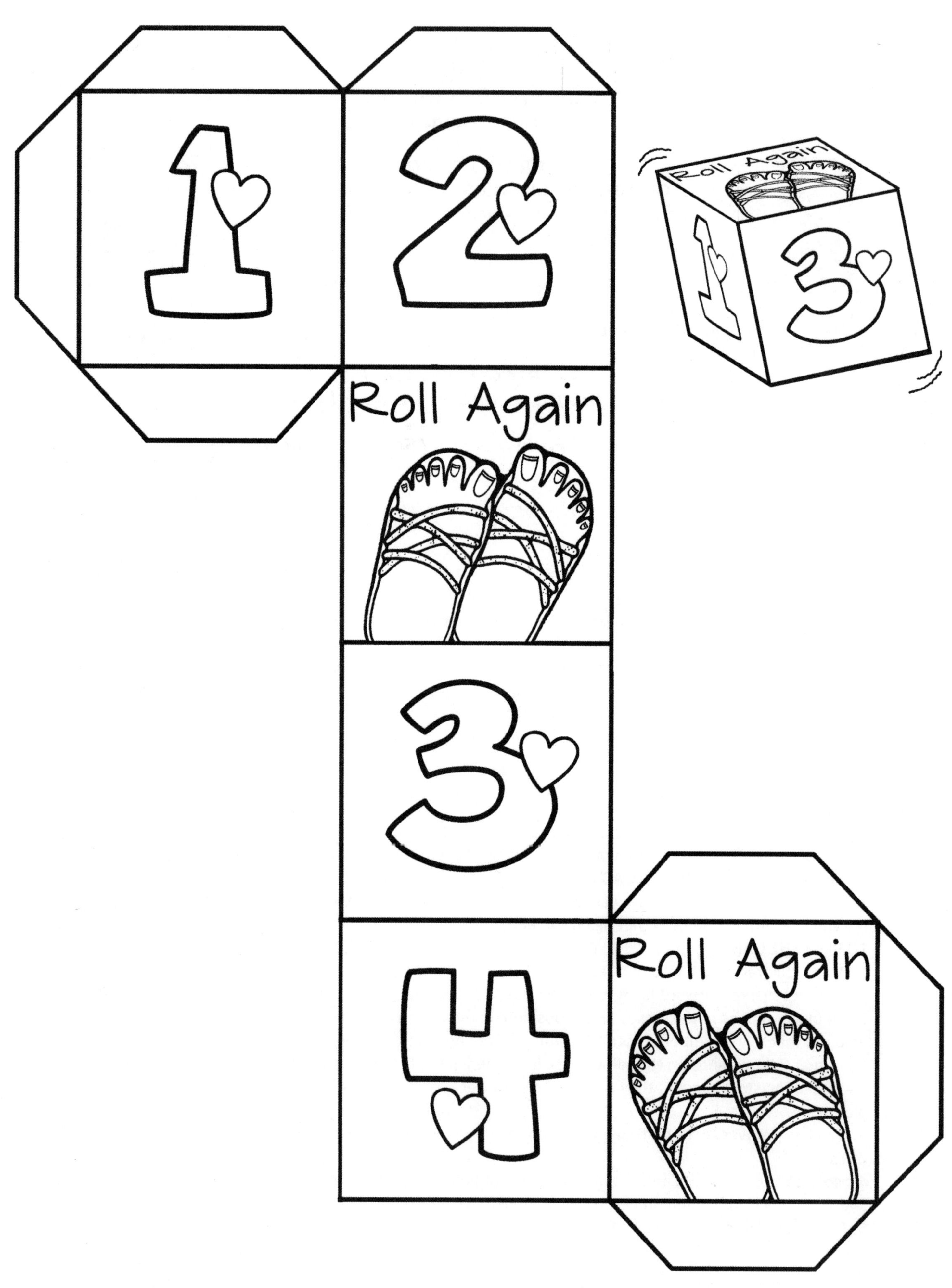

1
2
Roll Again
Roll Again
1
3
Roll Again
3
4
Roll Again

START
Mother is busy fixing dinner, and the baby is crying.
The neighbor's dog is lost.
A

Glue side A here.
1
Every day Grandmother goes out to her mailbox because she often feels lonely and likes to get mail.
2
B

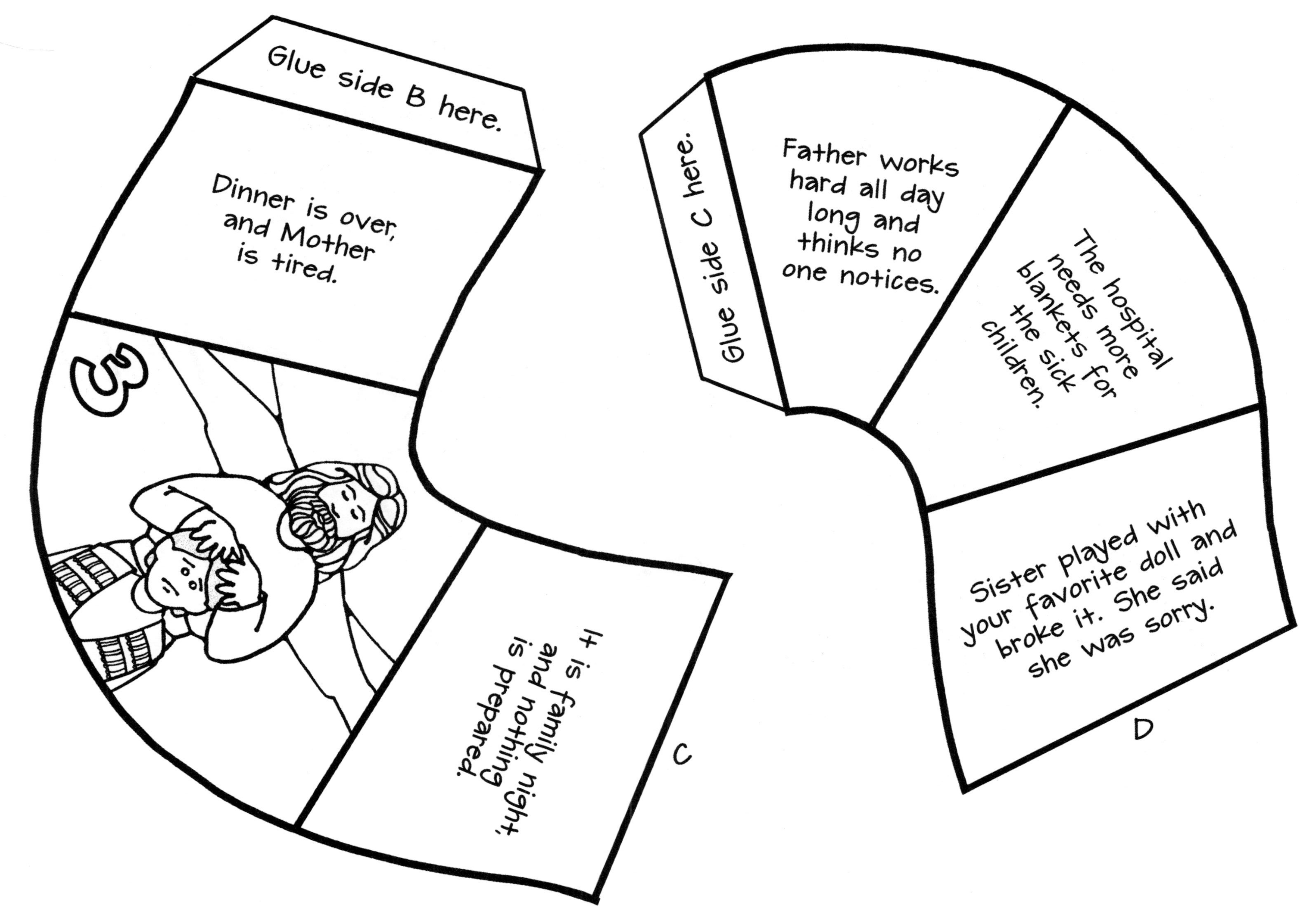
Glue side B here.
Dinner is over, and Mother is tired.
3
It is family night, and nothing is prepared.
C
Glue side C here.
Father works hard all day long and thinks no one notices.
The hospital needs more blankets for the sick children.
Sister played with your favorite doll and broke it. She said she was sorry.
D

Glue side D here.
4
Little brother can't read but wants to hear a story.
5
A boy in your school class does not have a coat for winter.
E

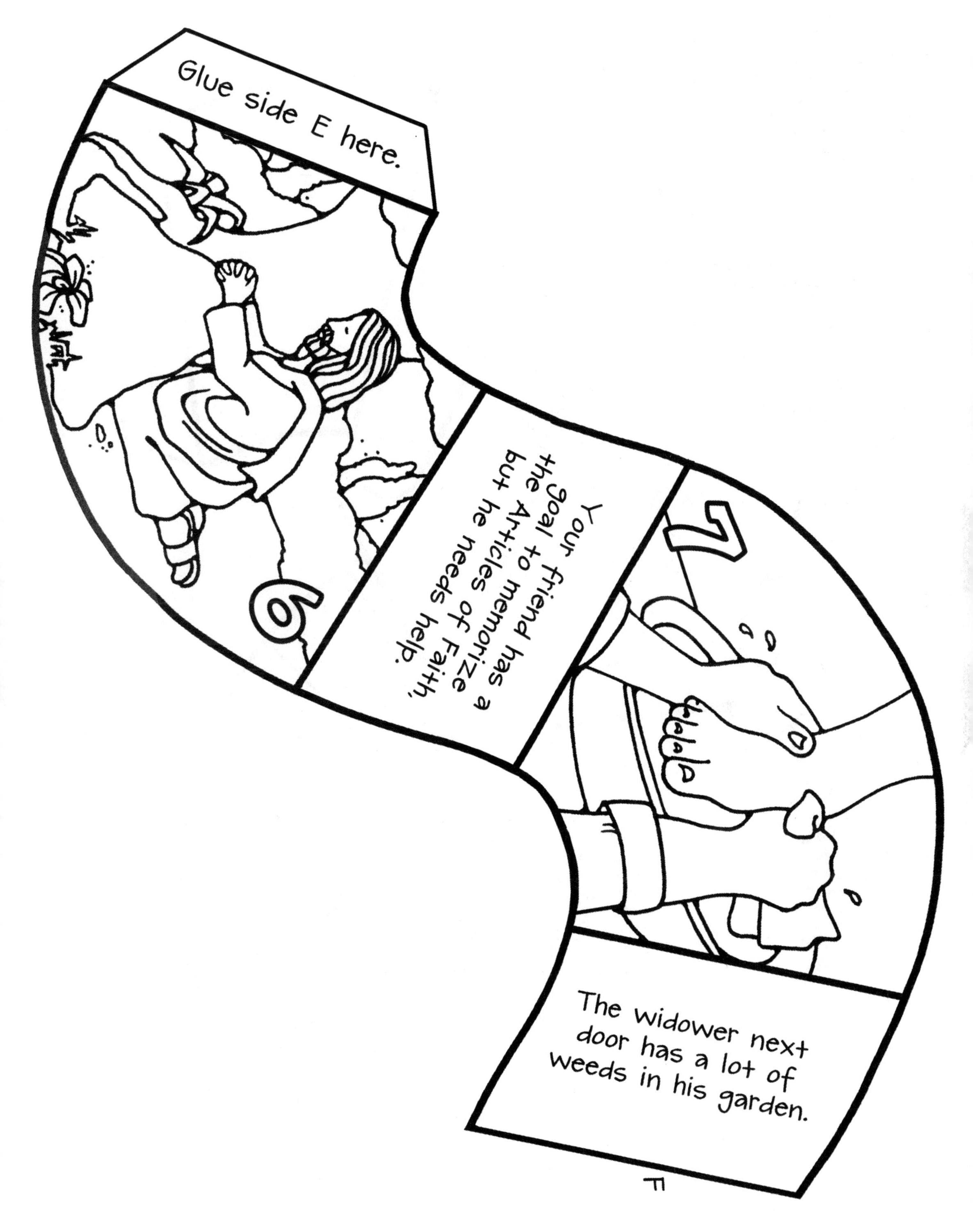
Glue side E here.
6
Your friend has a goal to memorize the Articles of Faith, but he needs help.
7
The widower next door has a lot of weeds in his garden.

F

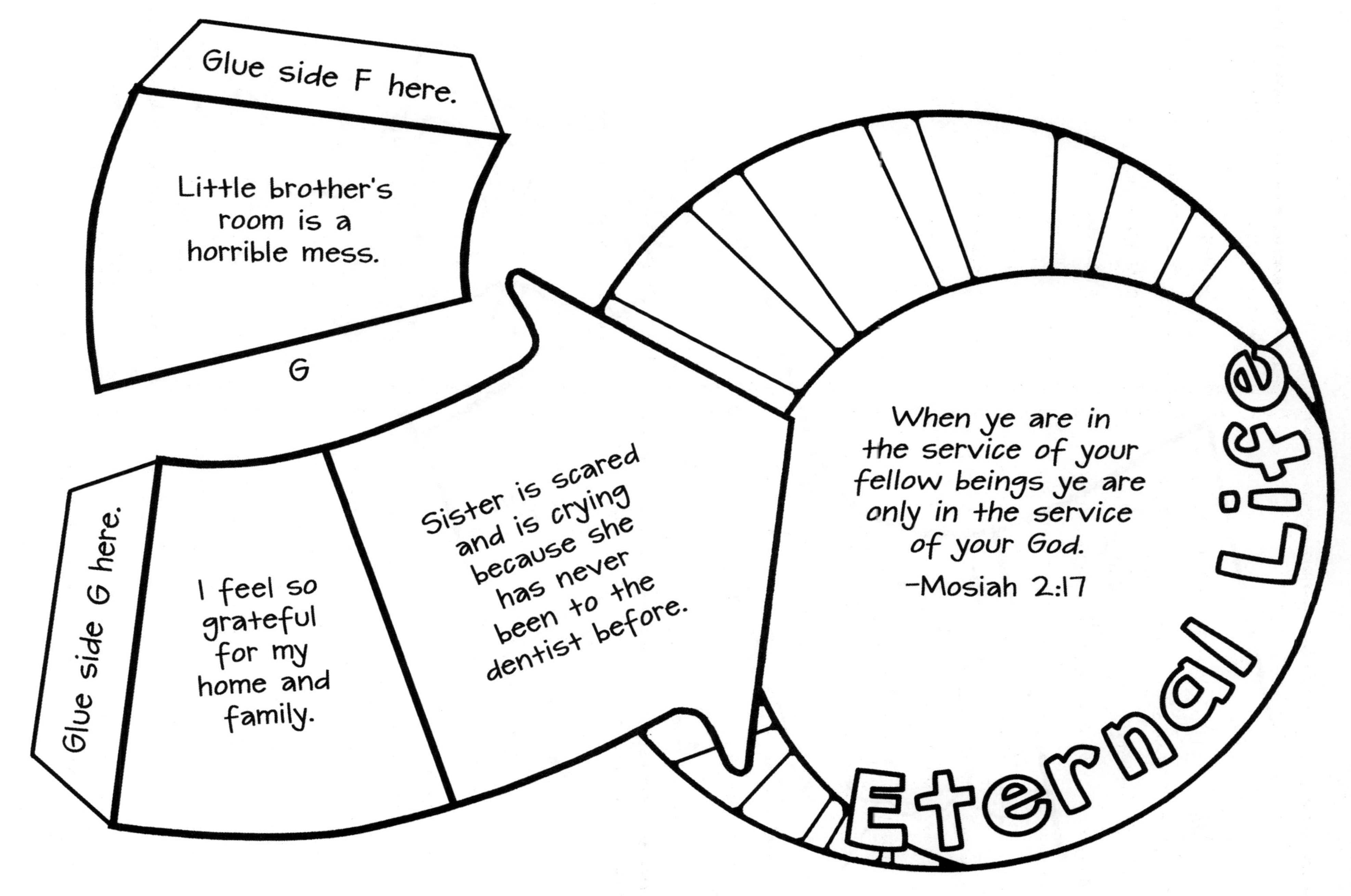
Glue side F here.
Little brother's room is a horrible mess.
G
Glue side G here.
I feel so grateful for my home and family.
Sister is scared and is crying because she has never been to the dentist before.
When ye are in the service of your fellow beings ye are only in the service of your God.
–Mosiah 2:17
Eternal Life

# Jesus Service Stories

## #1 Sermon on the Mount

Jesus went up on a high mountain, and thousands of people gathered to hear Him. He taught them the Beatitudes so they could learn to be happy. He taught them to be kind, to forgive, and to love others. He taught them how they can go back to heaven.

LIKE JESUS, WE SHOULD NOT BE AFRAID TO TELL OTHERS ABOUT THE GOSPEL.

## #2 Jesus Feeds 5,000

When Jesus was teaching thousands of people on the mountain, He taught them all day until it was night. The people wanted to stay to hear more, but they were also hungry and had not brought food. Jesus told His disciples to go look for food. They only found five loaves of bread and two fish—not enough to feed 5,000. So, Jesus blessed the bread and fish and broke it into pieces. The disciples took the people food and there was more than enough to feed all of them; this was a miracle.

LIKE JESUS, WE CAN CARE ENOUGH AND SHARE OUR FOOD WITH THOSE IN NEED.

## #3 Jesus Heals a Blind Man

One day Jesus was walking with His disciples,  and they saw a blind man. His disciples thought the man was born blind because he or his parents had sinned. Jesus said they had not sinned. He said the man was born blind so that Jesus could heal him and show God's power. Jesus had a special power from God called the priesthood. He made mud out of dirt and put it on the man's eyes. Jesus told him to wash his eyes. When the man obeyed he could see. The man had faith and was healed.

LIKE JESUS, WE CAN HELP THE SICK.

## #4 Jesus Heals Ten Lepers

Jesus went to a small town, where he saw ten men who were lepers. They had sores all over their bodies and their skin was falling off. Doctors could not help them, and people would not go near them or they would get sick too. The lepers asked Jesus to heal them, to make their sores go away. Jesus listened to them, and He wanted them to get well. He told them to go to the priests, and they obeyed. On the way to the priests, their sores disappeared; Jesus had healed them. One man came back, knelt down, and thanked Jesus for healing him.

LIKE JESUS, WE CAN CARE FOR OTHERS. LIKE THE ONE LEPER WHO GAVE THANKS, WE CAN GIVE THANKS TO JESUS AND OTHERS.

## #5 Jesus Blesses the Children

One day Jesus was with His disciples and He was very tired. Some people wanted Jesus to bless their children, and the disciples told them not to bring them to Jesus. Jesus told His disciples to bring the children to Him. He told them they should love little children and they should have faith like little children. Jesus took the time to bless the children, and the children loved Jesus very much.

LIKE JESUS, WE CAN LOVE AND CARE FOR OTHERS, ESPECIALLY CHILDREN AND THE ELDERLY.

## #6 Jesus Suffers in the Garden

At the end of His mission, Jesus went to the Garden of Gethsemane with His Apostles. He asked most of them to wait, but he asked three to come with Him while He went to pray. The three went to sleep because Jesus prayed for a very long time. Jesus came back and asked them to stay awake. Jesus prayed and was very sad. He began to shake and blood came out of His skin. His body hurt as He suffered for all of the sins of all people. Angels came to help make Him stronger. Jesus did not want to suffer, but He knew this must be done to obey Heavenly Father.

LIKE JESUS, WE CAN OBEY ALL OF HEAVENLY FATHER'S COMMANDMENTS.

## #7 Jesus Washes His Apostles Feet

Jesus and His Apostles wore sandals instead of shoes. One day they came back very tired from walking, and their feet were sore and dirty. Jesus filled a bowl with water and wanted to wash Peter's feet. Peter said he did not want Jesus to wash his feet. Jesus said that if He could not wash Peter's feet, Peter could not be a "part" of Jesus. Peter then said he wanted Jesus to wash his feet, because he wanted to be His friend.

LIKE JESUS, WE CAN SERVE OTHERS, SHOWING OUR LOVE.

## SEPTEMBER Theme: I WILL SERVE GOD WITH ALL MY HEART, MIGHT, MIND, AND STRENGTH

***PRACTICE TIME (download scripture & song visuals shown on p. 90 from GospelGrabBag.com)***

### *SHARING TIME, Weeks 3–4: When I serve others, I serve God.*

### *ACTIVITY: Love and Serve Others (Lovey's Service Station)*

**OBJECTIVE:** Help children think of simple acts of service they can do each day at home, school, and at church, and learn that true happiness comes from serving others.

**TO MAKE:** Copy, color, and cut out the images and word strips that follow. You'll need 12 cars (make three copies). Mount the service station parts on a poster as shown and laminate the entire poster. Glue situations on the back of cars, then laminate cars and cut out. Mount the broken cars around the room. *Option:* Find picture of Jesus washing the Apostles' feet.

**ACTIVITY:**

1. Tell children, "Heavenly Father and Jesus want us to serve and help others without asking for something in return. He knows that this is the only way we can be happy. When Jesus was on the earth, He washed the feet of the Apostles (John 13:1–7). They wore sandals, and their feet were dusty and dirty. Jesus wanted to serve them because of His love for them. Through this service they knew Jesus love them. We too can show our family, friends, neighbors, and those at Church that we care about them. Let's find cars that need repair and people that need care and take them to ***Lovey's Service Station*** to learn how we can fix their cars, help them, and send them on their way." Demonstrate by moving a car to a station in front at the ***Jalopy "Junk"tion*** sign, then move it to the ***Ready-to-roll!*** *sign.*

2. Have children take turns choosing a car, reading the description, and parking it in front of the ***Jalopy "Junk"tion*** sign. The description tells the problem with the car and the person that is driving the car. As children drive their broken down cars to the ***Lovey's Service Station*** for repair, encourage them to have fun, e.g., make broken-down rough-engine noises (squeak, clank-clank).

3. Tell ways the Lovey's Service Station can repair the car and help the person driving the car. Then park (mount) the car in front of the ***Ready-to-Roll!*** sign for a second, then drive them off, making "zoom" and "purring-engine" sounds.

4. Repeat until all cars are serviced and people served.

Do not cut along the dotted line. Use this margin to mount the other side.

Cut carefully along the inside of the dotted line.

Ready-to-Roll!
Jalopy "Junk"tion

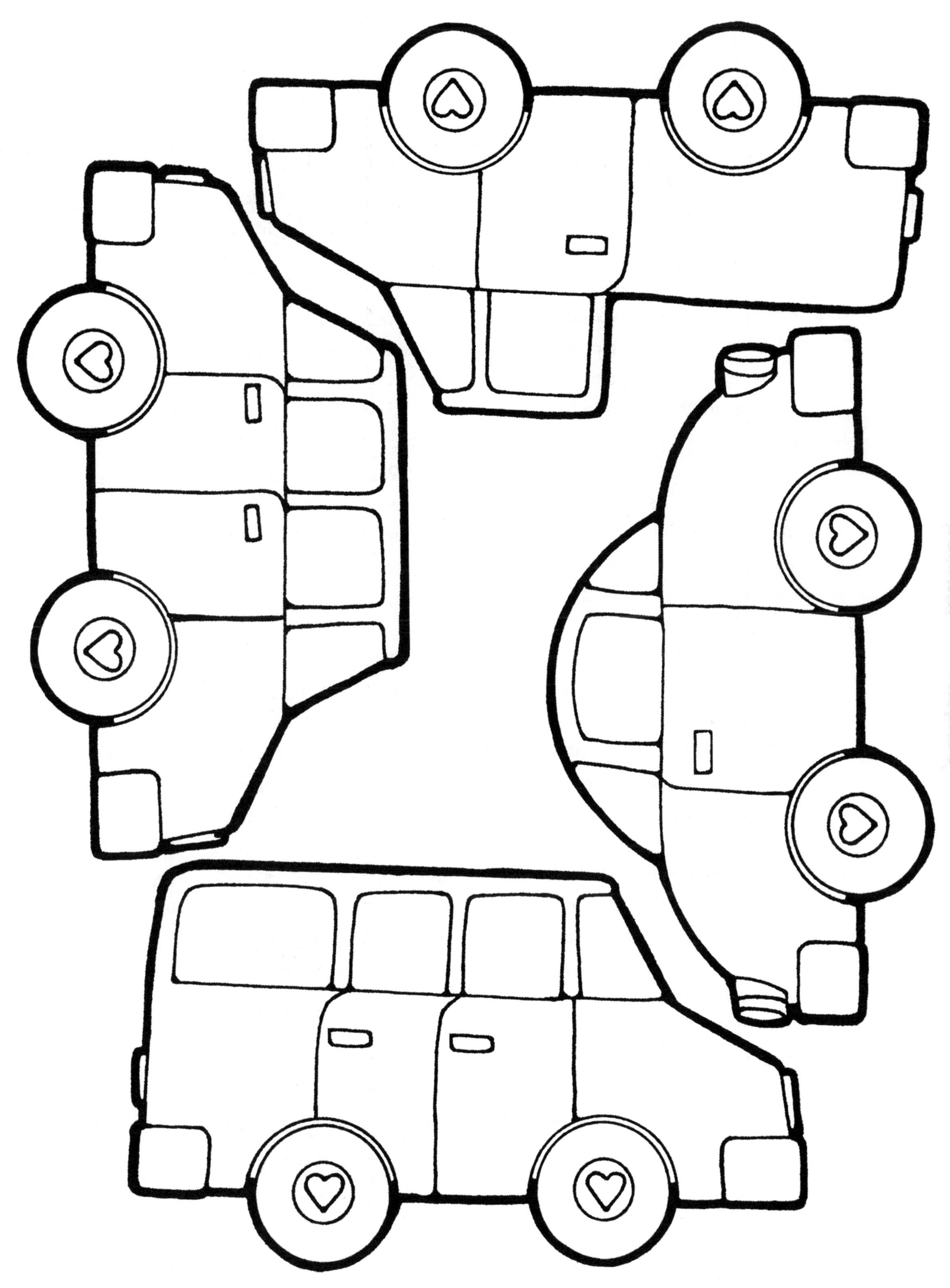

***Car Repair:*** *Flat Tire*
***Person Care:*** Shelby was running home after school when she tripped and skinned her knee.

***Car Repair:*** *Broken Windshield*
***Person Care:*** Susie was playing ball in the school yard. Someone bumped her, and her glasses fell off and broke.

***Car Repair:*** *Tire Lost a Hubcap*
***Person Care:*** You were hurrying to get to your baseball game when you saw a person's wallet in the street.

***Car Repair:*** *Dirty*
***Person Care:*** You were walking your little brother to his best friend's party when a car splashed mud all over his new pants and shoes.

***Car Repair:*** *Overheated Radiator*
***Person Care:*** Your little sister needs someone to play with, and she is bugging you. You are about ready to lose your temper.

***Car Repair:*** *Missing Muffler*
***Person Care***: Your sister has friends over to hear her favorite music CD, and she can't find it.

***Car Repair:*** *Missing Tire*
***Person Care:*** The lady next door is searching for her little boy, who is missing.

***Car Repair:*** *Broken Headlight*
***Person Care:*** Your neighbor lost his watch while mowing the lawn, and it is too dark to see.

***Car Repair:*** *Broken Windshield* Wiper
***Person Care:*** Your brother smeared poster paint all over your dad's bathroom mirror; now he can't see to shave.

***Car Repair:*** *Broken Door Handle*
***Person Care:*** It was the biggest soccer game of the year. You were trying to help your best friend make the goal line when he tripped and broke his arm in two places.

***Car Repair:*** *Busted Radiator Hose*
***Person Care:*** It was raining hard outside when your mother yelled, "The basement is flooding!"

***Car Repair:*** *Ran Out of Gas*
***Person Care:*** Your little brother is crying because he is hungry, and your mom is not home to fix dinner.

## OCTOBER Theme: I Will Share the Gospel with All of God's Children

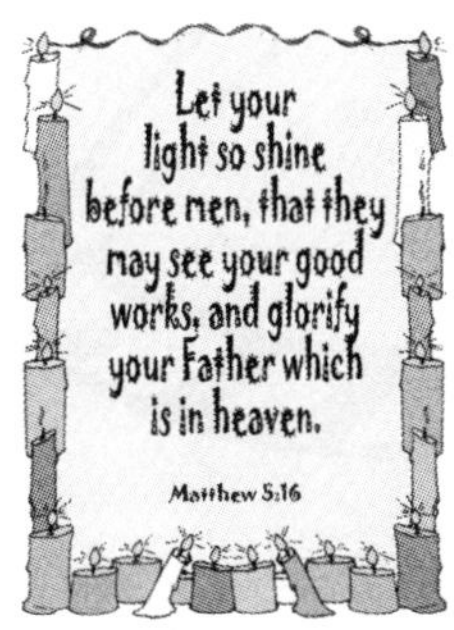


### *PRACTICE TIME:*

. **SCRIPTURE MEMORIZATION—Matthew 5:6** (shown left). Posters and cards are available to download from GospelGrabBag.com.
. **PRACTICE SONG—Sing "We'll Bring the World His Truth"** (*Children's Songbook*, 172) using the song visuals (shown right). These are available to download from GospelGrabBag.com.

### *SHARING TIME, Week 1:*
### *Living the gospel helps me be a missionary now.*

### *ACTIVITY: Fishers of Men (Missionary Fish-ionary Fish Find)*

**OBJECTIVE:** Help children learn the right (good fish-ionary) ways and the wrong (stinky fish-ionary) ways to be a missionary. Children can learn positive ways to share the gospel as they go fish.

**TO MAKE:** Copy, color, and cut out the images that follow. Laminate. Create a fishing pole and a fishing pond (with a sheet or tablecloth draped over chairs or easels. Tie a string to the left and right to drape good fish on the line as they are caught. Pin stinky fish below on the drape. Make "I can be a fisher of men" name badge for each child and write their name.

**ACTIVITY:** Read Matthew 4:19–20 (fishers of men). Tell children, "We can become fishers of men like Jesus." He called His disciples to follow Him and to teach the gospel. We too can follow Jesus and teach the gospel to be fishers of men. We can tell others about Jesus Christ's Church. Let's go fishing to find ways to be a good missionary fish-ionaries and how to avoid being stinky fish-ionaries.

TO PLAY:

1. Divide into two teams.
2. Take turns fishing (Primary leader paper clips a fish to string and yanks when fish is ready).
3. The child (or leader) reads fish aloud and tells if it is a good missionary or a stinky missionary action, then places the fish on the line (draped across the cloth) or tapes the stinky fish below.
4. Write one point earned each time a team chooses a good fish and hangs it up proudly. You might write the team's names on the board to record points. Team names might be "Tough Tunas," "Macho Mackerels," or "Courageous Catfish").
5. Give out name badges to each "Fish"ionary.

106–112 (Instructions & Visuals)

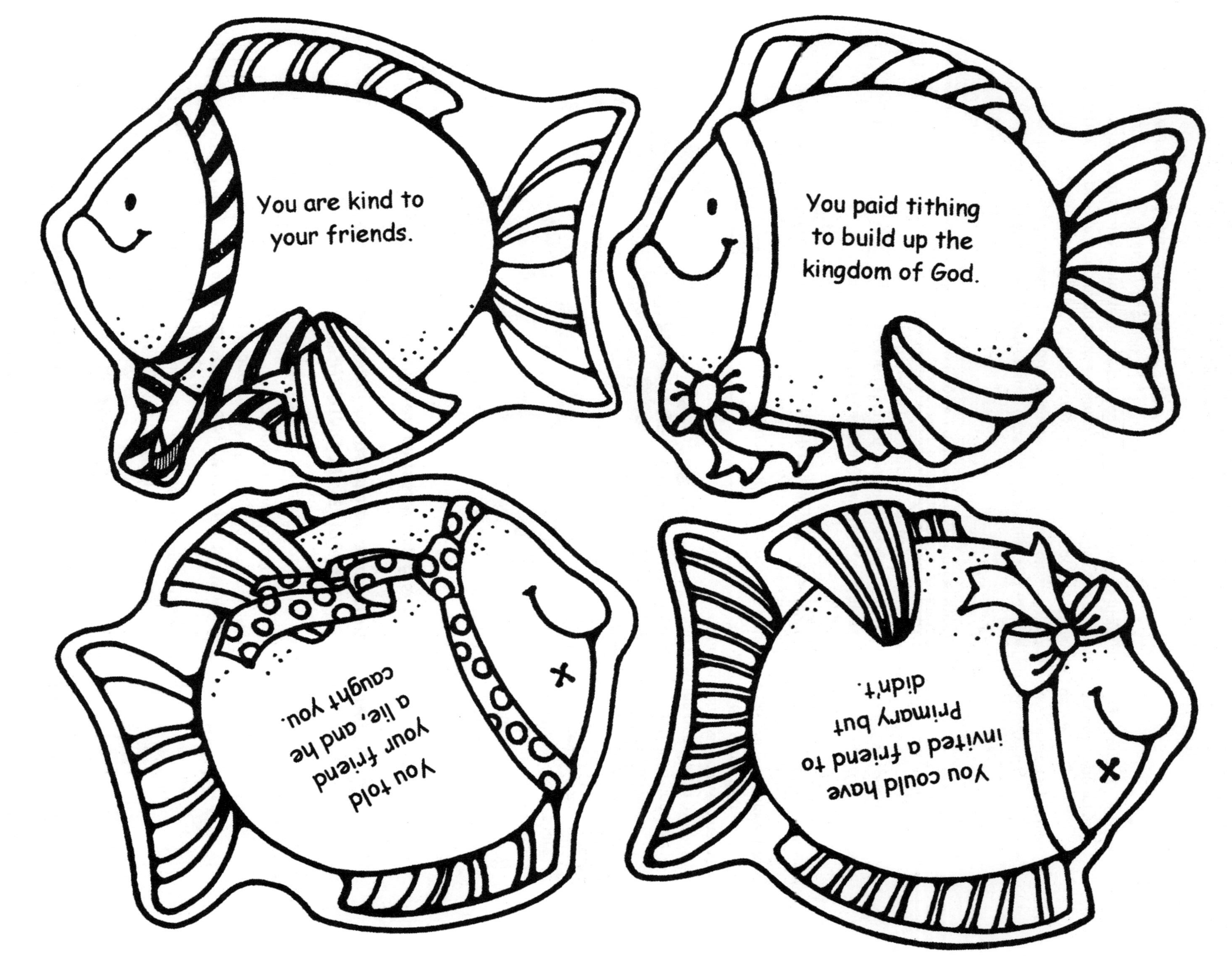
You are kind to your friends.
You paid tithing to build up the kingdom of God.
You told your friend a lie, and he caught you.
You could have invited a friend to Primary but didn't.

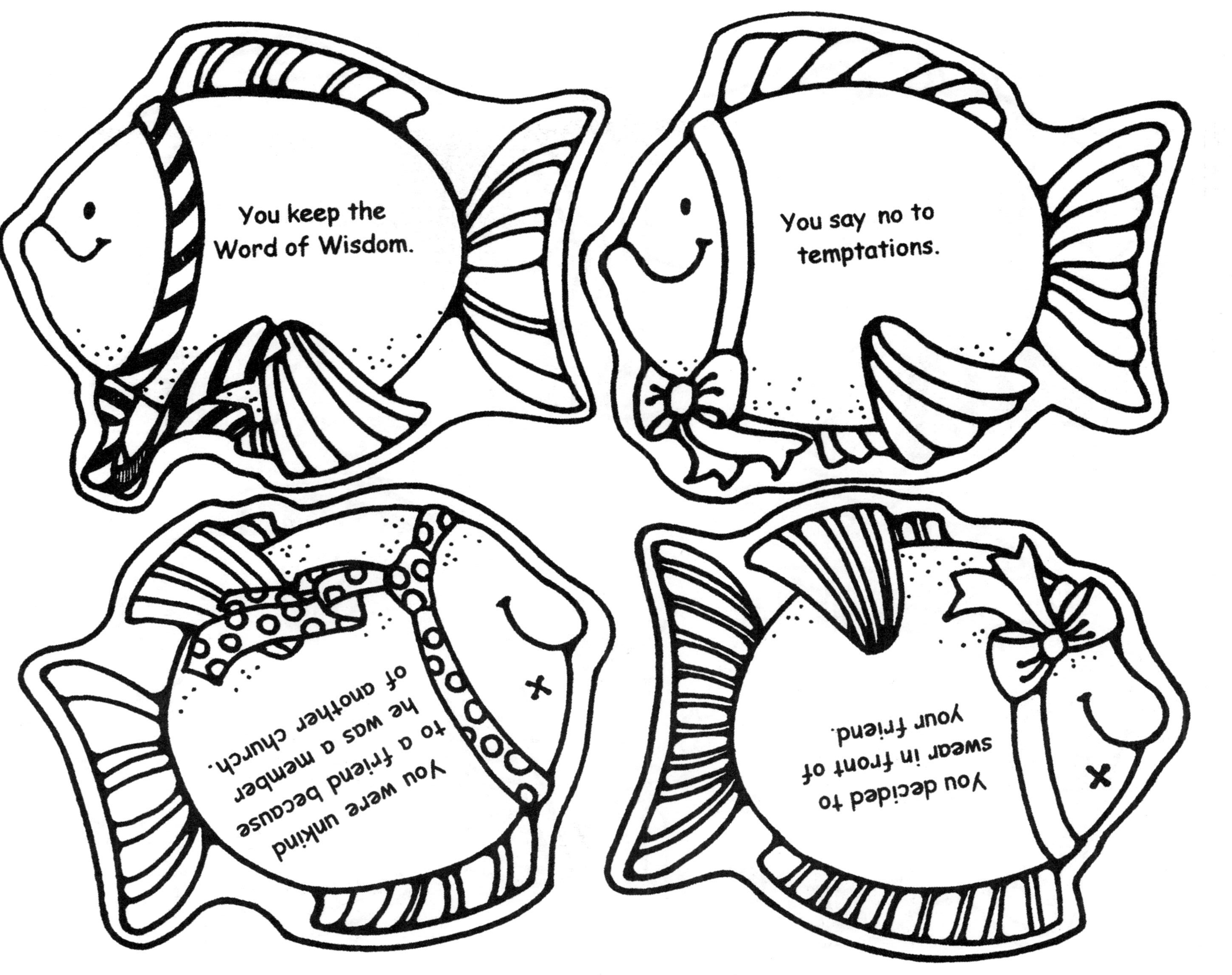
You keep the
Word of Wisdom.
You say no to
temptations.
You were unkind
to a friend because
he was a member
of another church.
You decided to
swear in front of
your friend.

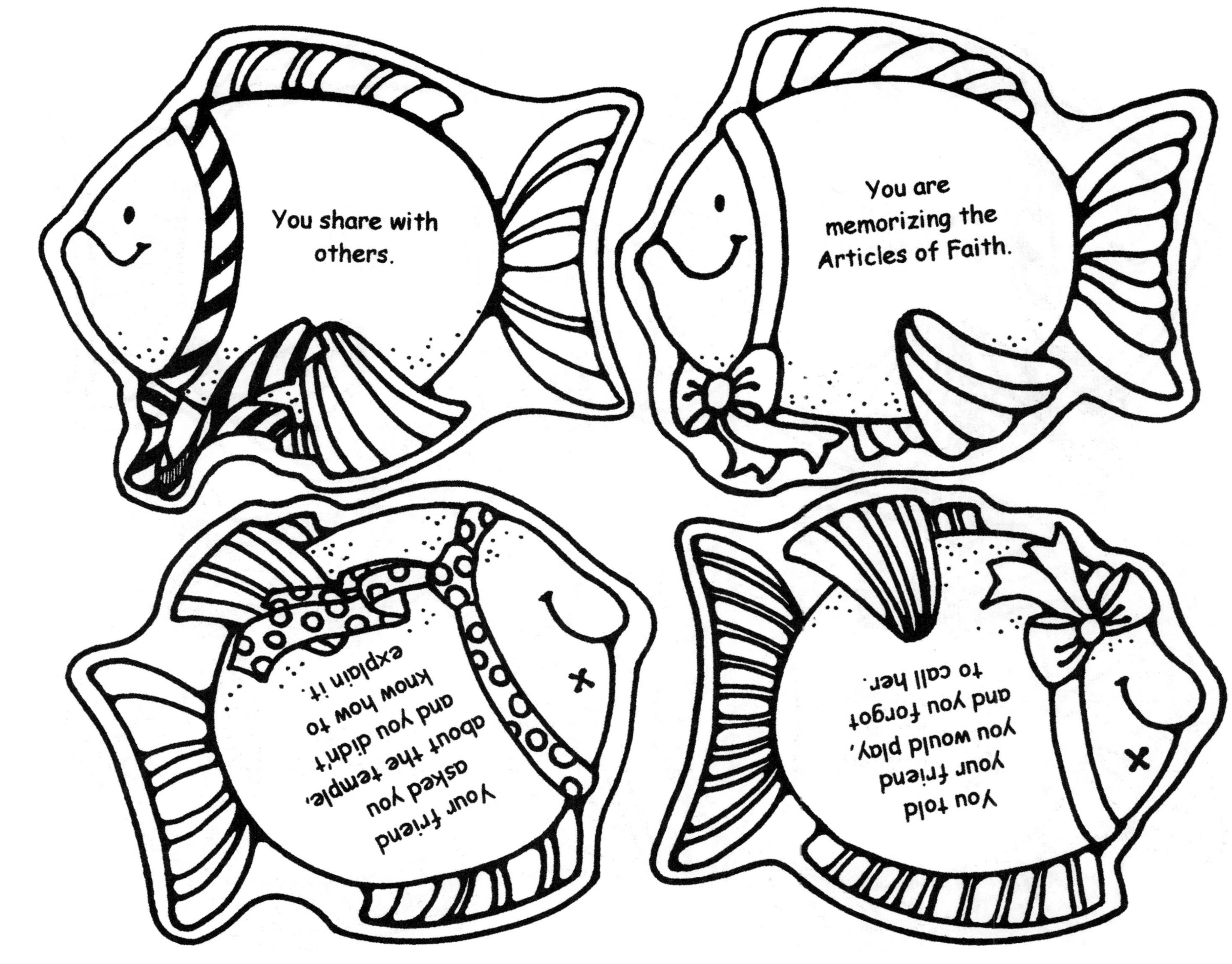

You share with others.
You are memorizing the Articles of Faith.
Your friend asked you about the temple, and you didn't know how to explain it.
You told your friend you would play, and you forgot to call her.

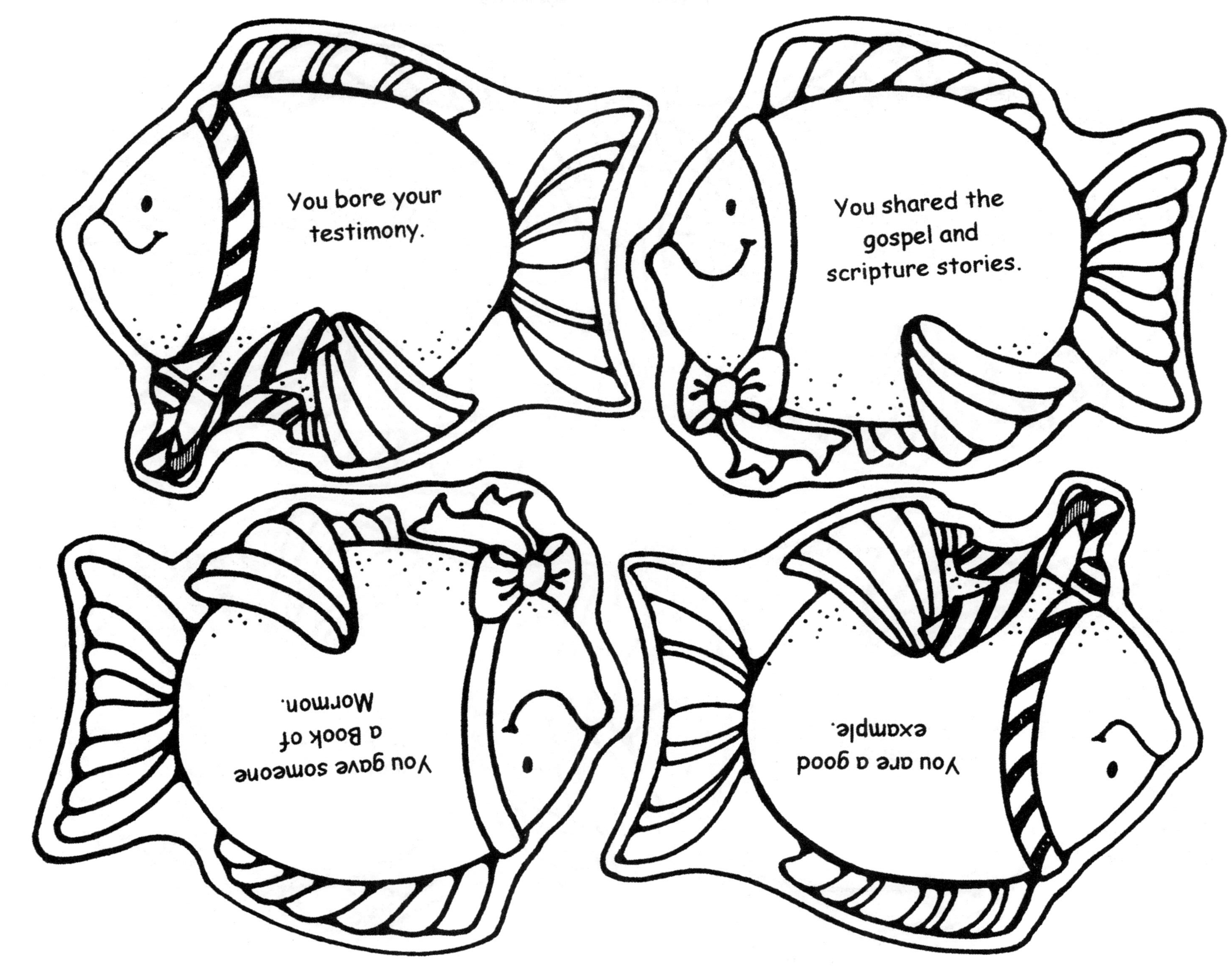
You bore your
testimony.
You shared the
gospel and
scripture stories.
You gave someone
a Book of
Mormon.
You are a good
example.

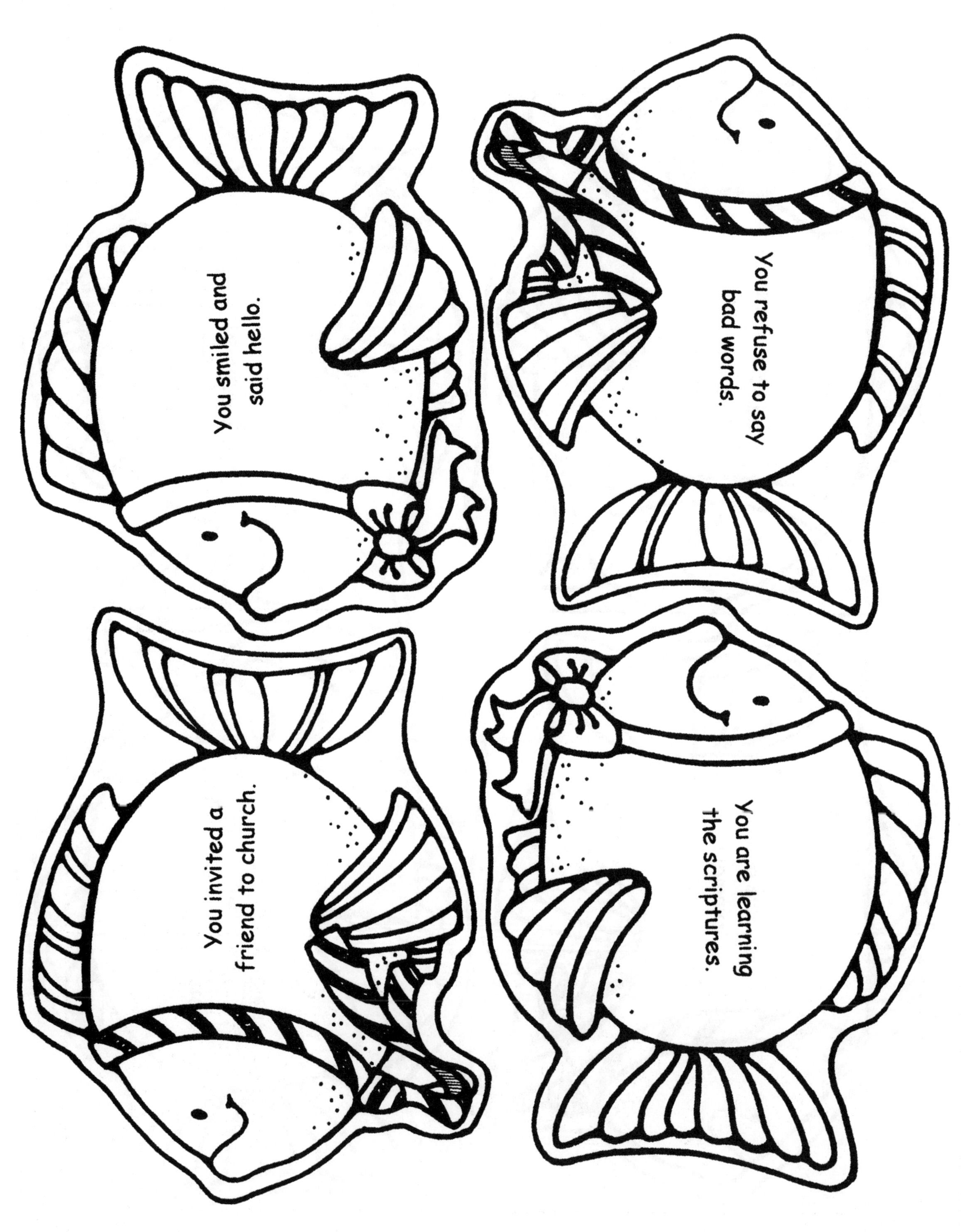
You smiled and said hello.
You refuse to say bad words.
You invited a friend to church.
You are learning the scriptures.

Name of Member "Fish"ionary

Name of Member "Fish"ionary

Name of Member "Fish"ionary

Name of Member "Fish"ionary

Name of Member "Fish"ionary

Name of Member "Fish"ionary

Name of Member "Fish"ionary

Name of Member "Fish"ionary

**OCTOBER Theme: I Will Share the Gospel with All of God's Children**

***PRACTICE TIME (download scripture & song visuals shown on p. 105 from GospelGrabBag.com)***

***SHARING TIME, Week 4:***
***My testimony is strengthened when I share the gospel.***

***ACTIVITY: I "Bee"-lieve (Sweet Testimony Sharing)***

**OBJECTIVE:**
Encourage children/youth to spontaneously bear their testimony about Jesus Christ, the Book of Mormon, temples (and forever families), Joseph Smith, the true Church, living prophets, and the priesthood.

**TO MAKE:** Copy, color, and cut out the images that follow. Laminate images. Have double-stick tape or magnets ready to post images on a poster or the board.

**ACTIVITY:**
Tell children, "Heavenly Father sent us to this earth with a testimony of His plan and of the gospel of Jesus Christ, but when we came, a veil was placed over our minds so we could not remember our life with Them. This way we would have to learn to live by faith. When we hear truth, the Holy Ghost will let us know. We will feel a warm feeling in our heart, and our mind will know that it is true. When we read the scriptures or hear others bear their testimony, we can know that what they say is true, especially if we pray for the Spirit to be with us."

Ask children, "Have any of your friends asked you about your church, about what you believe in?" Point to the sign and say, "Let's have an ***I 'Bee'-lieve Sweet Testimony*** Sharing Time. Come up and grab a bee and place it on the picture about which you wish to bear your testimony. Then buzz your sweet testimony so we can hear. This will help you practice for when you bear, or buzz, your testimony to your family and friends or in testimony meeting.

The Book of Mormon
Another Testament of Jesus Christ
True Church

Cut carefully along inside of dotted line.

e”-lieve . . .

Scrumptious Sharing

Do not cut along dotted line.
Use this margin to mount other side.

## NOVEMBER Theme: We Are to Thank God in All Things

### *PRACTICE TIME:*

**. SCRIPTURE MEMORIZATION—Mosiah 18:23** (shown left). Posters and cards are available to download from GospelGrabBag.com.

**. PRACTICE SONG—Sing "Thanks to Our Father"** (*Children's Songbook*, 20) using the song visuals (shown right). These are available to download from GospelGrabBag.com.

### *SHARING TIME, Weeks 2 and 3:*
### *I am thankful for temporal blessings / spiritual blessings.*

### *ACTIVITY: Don't Just Gobble Up Blessings*
### *(Extra-Miler Thankful Turkey Feather Find)*

**OBJECTIVE:** Give children an opportunity to give thanks for promised blessings, and tell them how they can truly show their gratitude by going the extra mile.

**TO MAKE:** Copy, color, and cut out the images that follow. Flip a poster to landscape position, and mount the turkey on the bottom of the poster; then laminate the entire poster. Laminate and cut out the turkey feathers. Ahead of time, place feathers around the room with double-stick tape or magnets.

**ACTIVITY:**

1. Show the picture from the ward library and tell the story of Jesus healing the ten lepers (Luke 17:12–19). Tell how one of the lepers came back to thank Jesus. He knew Jesus had healed him, and he knelt down and thanked Jesus for making him well. Heavenly Father has promised us many blessings if we are faithful in keeping His commandments. As those blessings come to us, we need to say thanks.
2. Show the turkey on the poster and say, "Let's not be a 'turkey' and just gobble up blessings. Let's remember where our blessings come from and go the extra mile like this turkey. Let's spread our feathers and give thanks. Let's talk about blessings our Heavenly Father has promised us and how we can give thanks."
3. Have children take turns coming up and finding a feather. Have them tell why they are thankful for the promised blessing (e.g., FAMILY) and place the feather on the turkey.
4. Then have that child choose another child to come up and help. Now tell them how they can go the extra mile (point to the tennis shoes on the turkey) and show their gratitude (e.g., with FAMILY, you can show you love them by helping them).

119–125 (Instructions & Visuals)

Cut carefully along the inside of the dotted line.

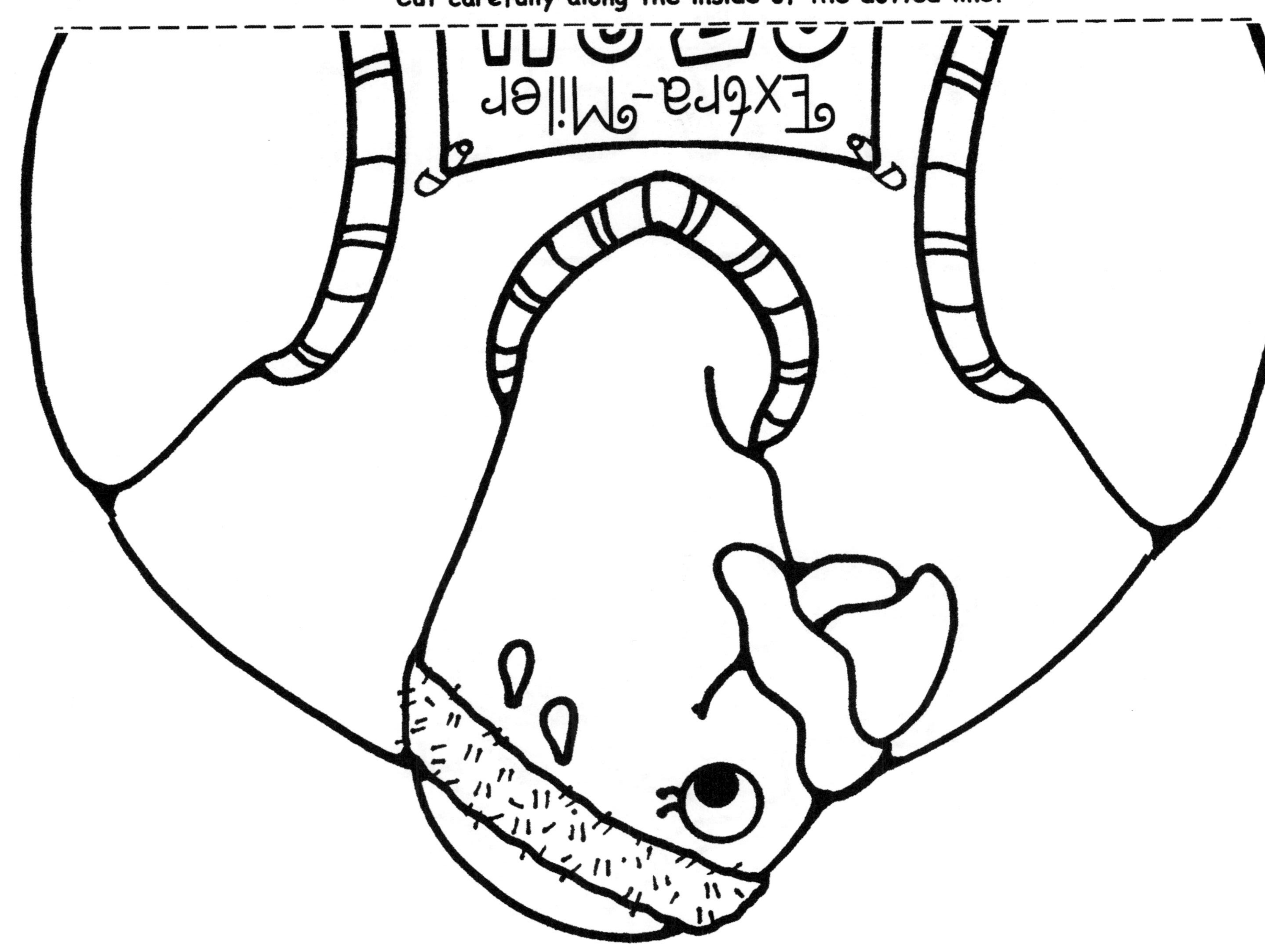

Do not cut along the dotted line. Use this margin to mount the other side.

2784

Prophets
Home
Eternal Family
Health
Holy Ghost
Baptism

Temples
Priesthood
CHILI
PEACHES
Food
Clothing
Friends
Talents

Forgiveness
Knowledge
Eternal Life
Testimony
Atonement
Scriptures

Happiness
Family Home Evening
Trials
Prayer
Animals
Primary Songs

## DECEMBER Theme: I Know That Jesus Christ Will Come Again

### *PRACTICE TIME:*

. **SCRIPTURE MEMORIZATION—Job 19:25** (shown left). Posters and cards are available to download from GospelGrabBag.com.

. **PRACTICE SONG—Sing "When He Comes Again"** (*Children's Songbook*, 82) using the song visuals (shown right). These are available to download from GospelGrabBag.com.

### *SHARING TIME, Week 2:*
### *Jesus Christ will come to the earth again.*

### *ACTIVITY: The World Will Know Peace*
### *("Lamb and Lion" Millennium Match Game)*

**OBJECTIVE:** Help children imagine what it will be like when Jesus returns, bringing 1,000 years of peace to the earth.

**TO MAKE:** Copy, color, and cut out the images that follow. Before laminating, write the letters A–P on the back of each lamb and lion so youth can call out the letters. Randomly mount images facedown on the board, with the lambs on the left and the lions on the right.

**PLAY THE GAME:**

1. Tell youth that before Jesus ascended into heaven, He told His Apostles that He would return to our Heavenly Father until the time of His Second Coming. When He returns again, He will return to the temple and bring in the Millennium. The Millennium is the thousand-year period when Jesus will reign on the earth. This will be a time of peace, when Satan will be bound. Evil will not have power. Even "the lamb shall lie down with the lion." Place a lamb and lion on the board, and talk about the difference between these two animals: the lamb is gentle and small, and the lion is large and dangerous. But when the Millennium comes, "the lamb shall lie down with the lion," which means there will be peace everywhere.

2. Talk about or sing the fourth verse in "The Spirit of God" (*Hymns,* 2), which talks about the lamb and the lion lying down together without any ire.

3. Tell youth, "Let's play the 'Lamb and Lion' Millennium Match game to learn what will happen in the thousand years of peace when Jesus will reign on the earth."

4. Divide youth into teams, and have them take turns turning cards over and reading the Millennial event to make a match. Tell them, "The first part of the sentence is on a lamb, and the second part of the sentence is on a lion."

5. Youth can come up and point to a lamb and lion to make a match, or they can call out a letter (*A–P* written on the back of each lamb or lion) to identify their choices (e.g., child can call out a letter from the lion side and a letter from the lamb side to make a match).

6. When a match is made, take the lamb and lion off and tape them to the side of the board away from the game.

7. Tell youth that after the Millennium, Satan will be set free for a short time, and some people will turn away from Heavenly Father. Satan will build armies. The angels and hosts of heaven will cast him out forever. Then all of the people who have ever lived on the earth will be judged and assigned to the kingdoms they have prepared for by how they have lived. The earth will be changed into the celestial kingdom (source: Gospel Principles, chapters 43, 44, 47).

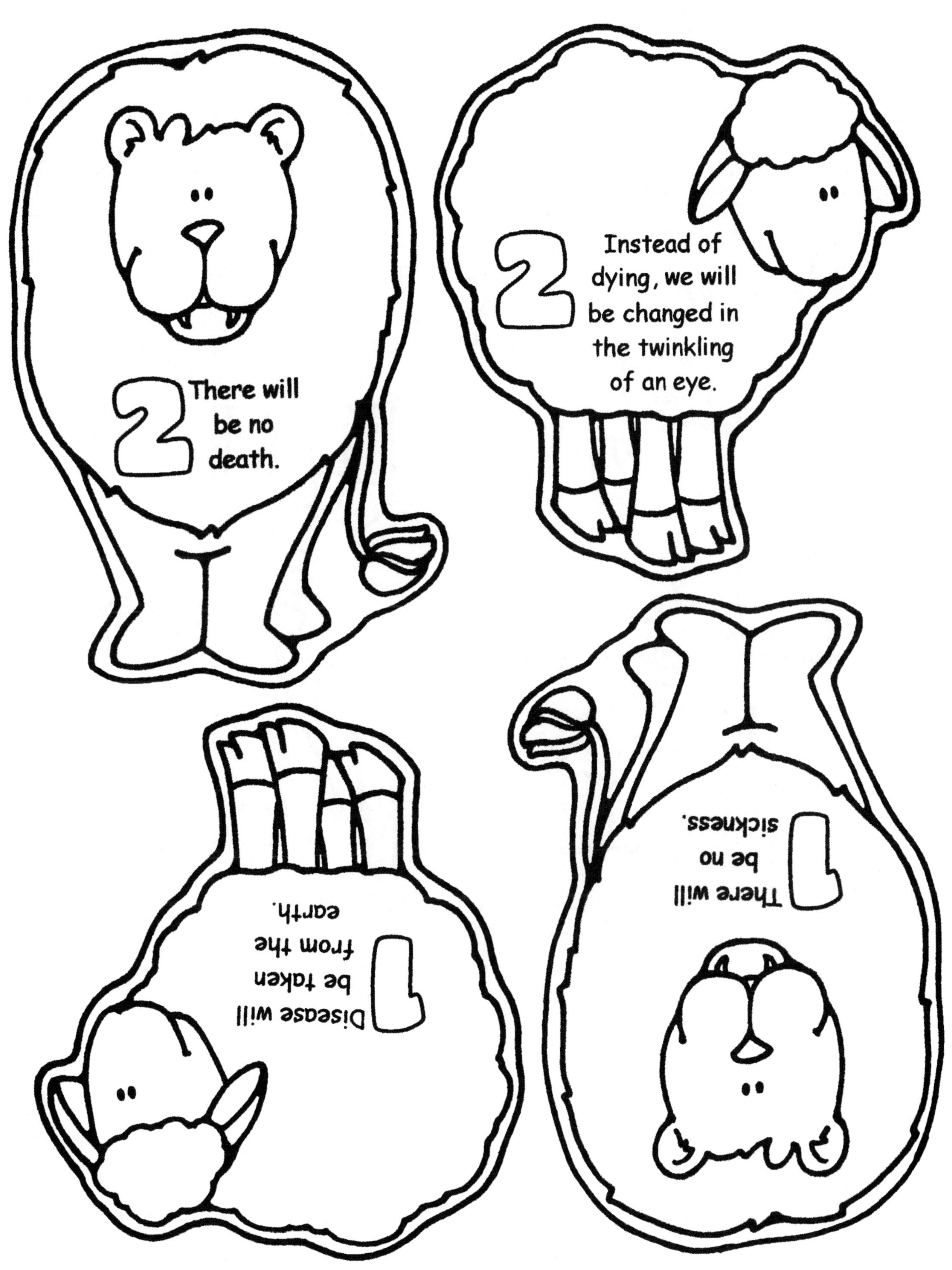
2
There will be no death.
2
Instead of dying, we will be changed in the twinkling of an eye.
1
Disease will be taken from the earth.
1
There will be no sickness.

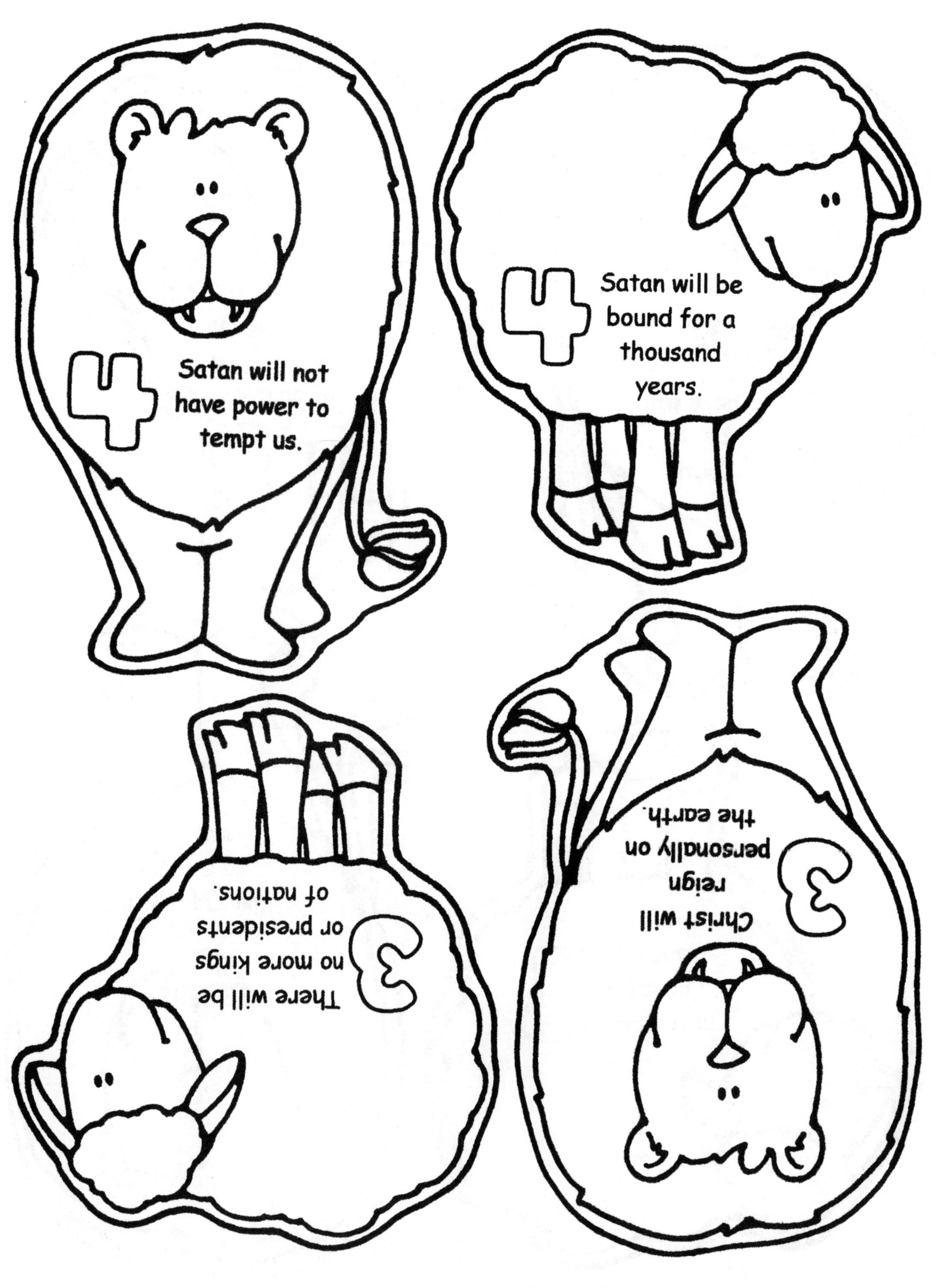
4
Satan will not have power to tempt us.
4
Satan will be bound for a thousand years.
3
There will be no more kings or presidents of nations.
3
Christ will reign personally on the earth.

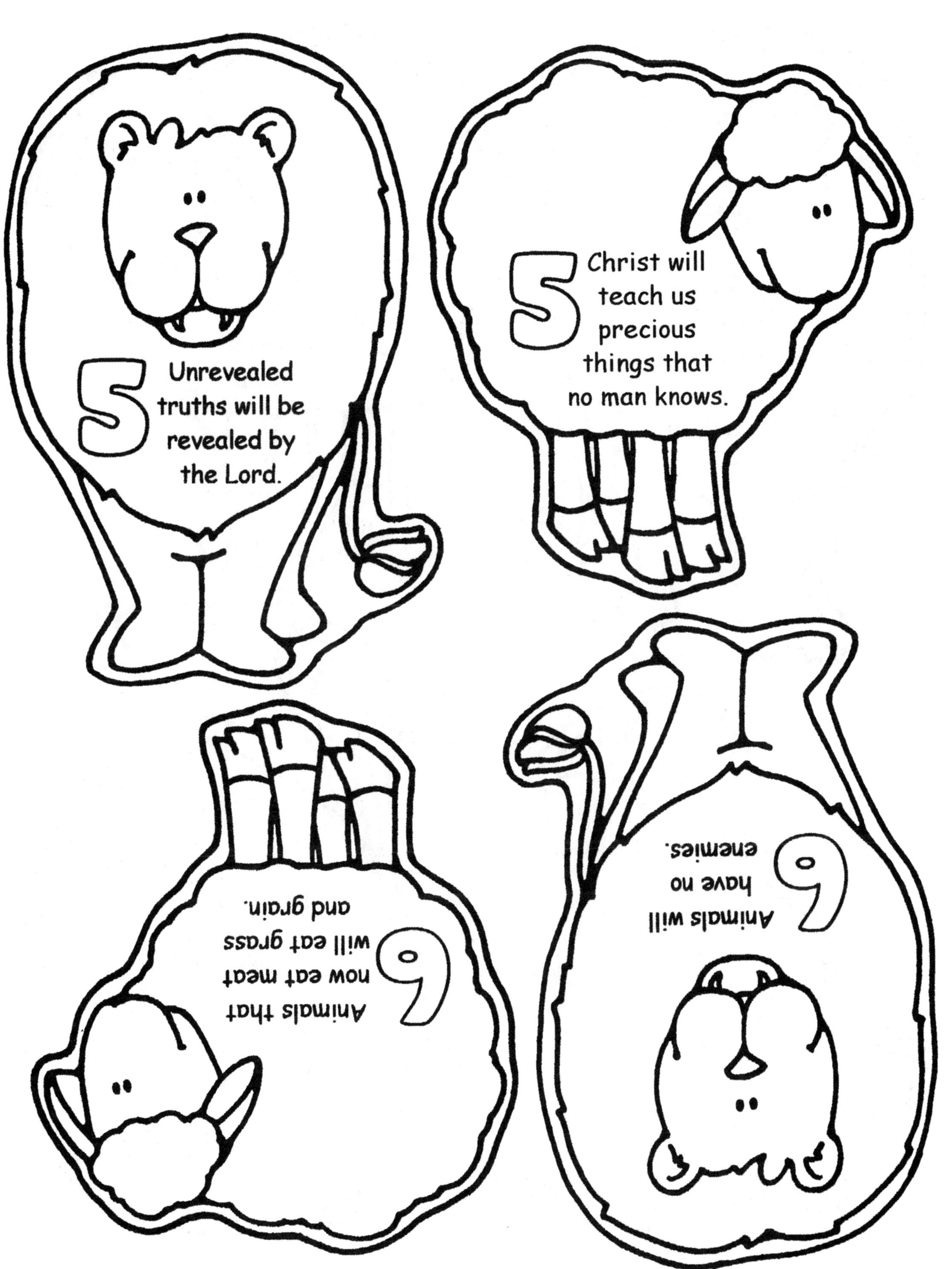
5 Unrevealed truths will be revealed by the Lord.
5 Christ will teach us precious things that no man knows.
6 Animals that now eat meat will eat grass and grain.
6 Animals will have no enemies.

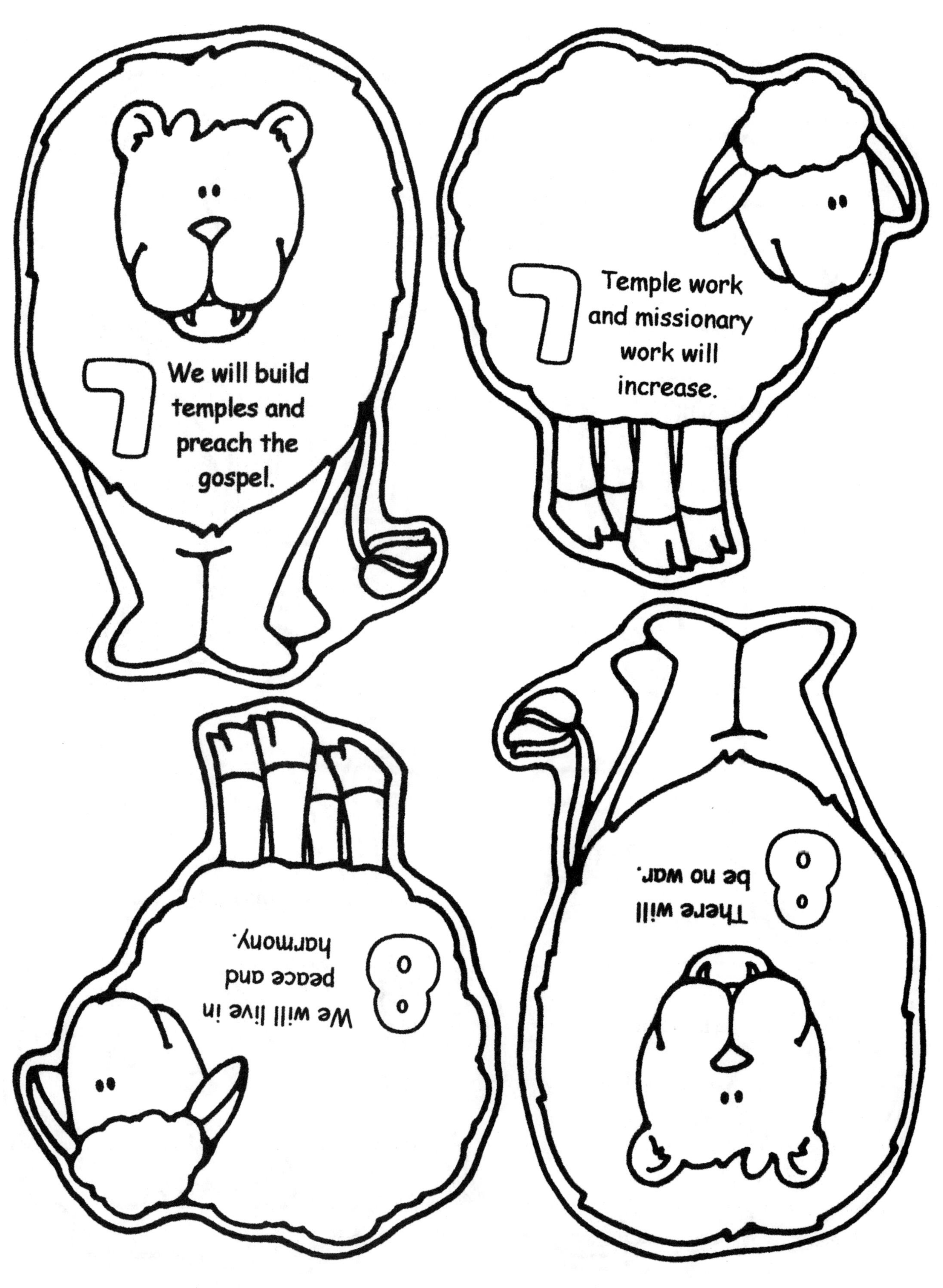
7
We will build temples and preach the gospel.
7
Temple work and missionary work will increase.
8
We will live in peace and harmony.
8
There will be no war.

## DECEMBER Theme: I Know That Jesus Christ Will Come Again

***PRACTICE TIME (download scripture & song visuals shown on p. 126 from GospelGrabBag.com)***

### *SHARING TIME, Week 3:*
### *I will prepare to live with Heavenly Father and Jesus Christ again.*

### *ACTIVITY: Second Coming Suitcase with Belongings*

**OBJECTIVE:** Show children how they can prepare to meet Jesus when He comes by packing their personal suitcase with things that will help them be the type of person Jesus would want to meet.

**TO MAKE:** Using cardstock, copy, color, and cut out the images that follow. Laminate. *Optional:* Mount suitcase right onto a poster, cutting a slit at the top of suitcase to insert items as you talk about them (gluing only the sides to a poster paper so the pocket remains open). Place suitcase items on the wall next to suitcase or around the room.

**TO PACK SUITCASE:** Tell children, "We are getting ready for a special day when Jesus Christ comes back to the earth. He wants us to be ready, so let's pack our bags."

1. Ask children one at a time to come up and find an item they could pack in their Second Coming suitcase.
2. Ask the child to read the message and talk about why this item would be important to pack (how it will prepare them to meet Jesus when He comes again), e.g., a pair of pants with patches on the knee to remind the child to "kneel in prayer."

**QUESTIONS:** Ask children the following:

***#1:*** What is the Second Coming? (When Jesus Christ comes again.)

***#2:*** What will it be like when Jesus comes again? (Jesus Christ will bring peace, happiness, and love among all righteous people.)

***#3:*** What can I do to prepare for the Second Coming when Jesus will come again? (Have faith and keep His commandments so that we will be ready to receive Him when He comes.)

↓ Cut carefully along inside of dotted line. ↓

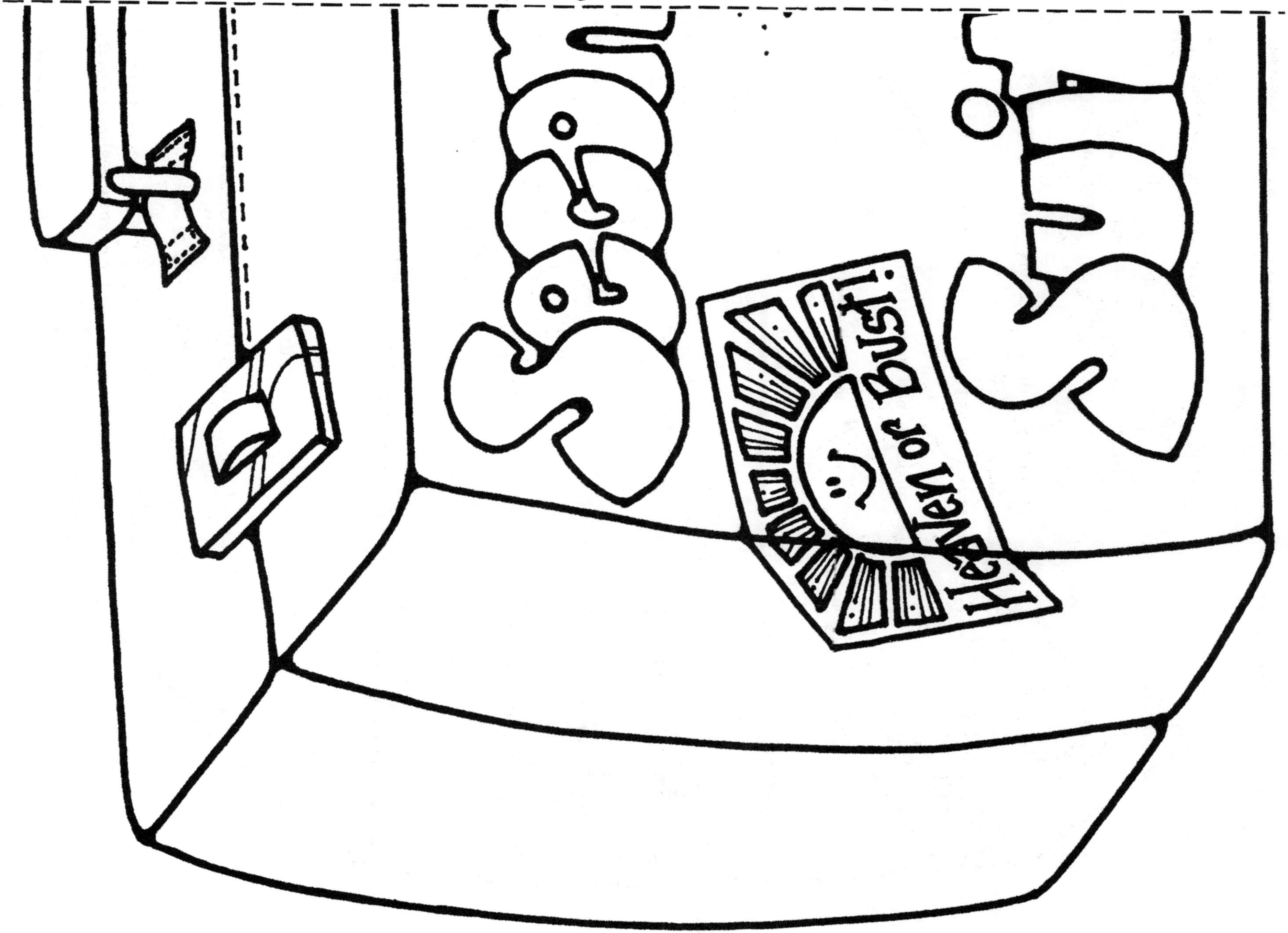

Heaven or Bust!

Do not cut along dotted line. Use this margin to mount other side.

dComing

case

I'm good to GO!

Dress modestly.
Kneel daily in prayer.
"Chews" the right.
Let your light shine, and share the gospel.
Use soothing words.

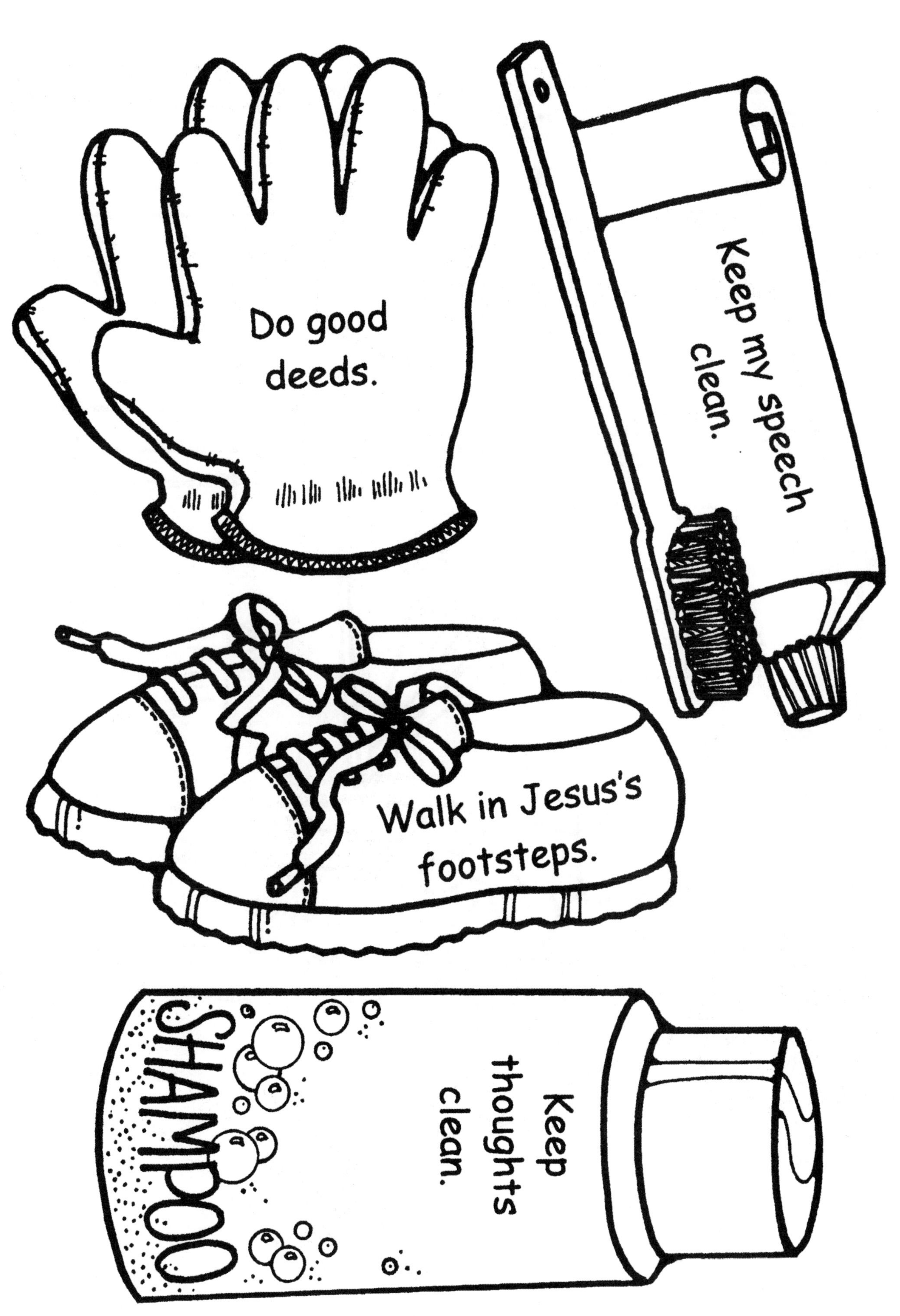
Do good deeds.
Keep my speech clean.
Walk in Jesus's footsteps.
SHAMPOO
Keep thoughts clean.

Obey
Word of
Wisdom.
GRANOLA
Prepare food
storage.
Read
scriptures.
Pay
tithing.
Repent to
stay clean.
Attend church.

I Am a Child of God
I Am a Child of God
I Am a Child of God
I Am a Child of God

I Am a Child of God

I Am a Child of God

I Am a Child of God

I Am a Child of God